The Art & Science of VITICULTURE and WINEMAKING

at the Williamsburg Winery

Williamsburg, Virginia

Settled Wessex Hundred 1617

The Williamsburg Winery is dedicated to blending age-old winemaking concepts with the advantages of modern technology to produce distinctive wines which reflect the Virginia tradition and quality of life.

MMXXI

The Art & Science of Viticulture and Winemaking
TABLE OF CONTENTS

PART 1

The Art and Science of Viticulture at the Williamsburg Winery

The Art and Science of Winemaking at the Williamsburg Winery

Barrels, Bottles and Corks

Advanced Technologies in Winemaking

A Listing of Regions, Wine Styles and Major Grape Varietals

Wine Aromas and Compounds

A Marriage of Wine and Food

PART 2

A History of Winemaking in Virginia

A Brief History of Wessex Hundred

The Williamsburg Winery at Wessex Hundred

Wine and Mathematics

The Wonders and Wisdom of New Technology in Winemaking

PART 3

Behind the Scenes at the Williamsburg Winery

The People at the Williamsburg Winery

The Places at the Williamsburg Winery

Epilogue

The Art & Science of
VITICULTURE and WINEMAKING
at the Williamsburg Winery

Great wine requires
a mad man to grow the vine,
a wise man to watch over it,
a lucid poet to make it,
and a lover to drink it.

–*Salvador Dalí*

Source: French poem seen on a wall in a hotel.

Copyright © 2021

All rights reserved. No part of this publication may be reproduced, distributed, or transmitted in any form or by any means, including photocopying, recording, or other electronic or mechanical methods, without the prior written permission of the publisher, except in the case of brief quotations embodied in critical reviews and certain other noncommercial uses permitted by copyright law. For permission requests, write to the publisher at 5800 Wessex Hundred, Williamsburg, Virginia 23185.

A NOTE FROM THE AUTHOR

Wine has been enjoyed for centuries. As a beverage, it can be delightfully simple, elegant, light, refreshing, rich, and full-bodied. Its structure is complex, and too often, that complexity can seem overwhelming. And yet, by definition, wine is merely fermented grape juice.

The sugar in the grapes turns into alcohol during fermentation, yielding a beverage that is at once both extremely stable—and in a state of becoming. As it ages, a wine may evolve to greatness—or well-deserved obscurity. An incredible number of variables affect the making of wine. The winemaker must consider them all, and then guide the process so that the end result will be a product that can be enjoyed at the table.

This booklet was designed to give visitors to the Williamsburg Winery some insights into the inspired art and the careful science that go into the making of fine wines.

This is the second edition of the Art and Science of Viticulture and Winemaking at the Williamsburg Winery. The first edition was produced in 2002, where 50,000 copies were appreciated by thousands of visitors.

It was noticed last year that used copies were still on sale on the internet.

The company has changed a lot since then!

This second edition is greatly enlarged and updated with full visuals in addition to including more comments on the world of wine and the creation of the winery. This issue also opens the door to the people who make this operation what it is. That section was written on the people and the places by Vicki L. Friedman, an independent and objective writer who enjoys the atmosphere of the winery and the friendliness of the folks who work here.

Yet, the most important thing we would have you remember is: TRUST YOUR OWN PALATE.

Drink what you enjoy; enjoy what you drink.

Above all, enjoy life!
Patrick G. Duffeler
Founder

The Entrance to Wessex Hall

INTRODUCTION BY JIM RAPER

Anyone who has known Patrick Duffeler as long as I have will remember hearing his basic wine appreciation advice, which goes something like this: "Trust your palate. Drink what you enjoy and enjoy what you drink." But we also know that behind this rather dispassionate statement is a man whose passion for wine has lifted him to enviable connoisseurship.

From my time spent with him in Virginia and France, I know he believes that enlightened enjoyment of wine comes to those who are willing to delve into the history and practices of grape growing and winemaking, into the characteristics of popular grape varieties and into the marvelous pairings possible for wine and food.

This brings us to the book you are reading, Patrick's "The Art & Science of Viticulture and Winemaking at the Williamsburg Winery." There are more comprehensive – and heavier – wine tomes in the marketplace, and in these pages you will find endorsements of the renowned wine writers Patrick admires, including the contemporary Brits Hugh Johnson, Jancis Robinson and Steven Spurrier. The goal of our author is to offer essential winemaking information in a compact book of breezy format.

Even if you already have a working knowledge of the general subject, Patrick adds insightful and intriguing content about how an itinerant, Belgium-born business executive came to plant his flag in Tidewater Virginia and found what has become the state's largest winery. There is no question that the Duffelers were pioneers in the creation of the modern Virginia wine industry.

Patrick has had a variety of life's experiences outside of wine. Here was a European who came to America for his formal education and then returned to embrace business ventures on the Continent. Space doesn't allow a full job history here; suffice it to say that he organized and directed Marlboro's entry into Formula One racing and later became a player in the France-based fragrance industry.

Wine, however, became an obsession over time. His business travels exposed him to some of the best restaurants in the world, as well as to celebrated wine regions. And, as if his other pursuits weren't fast track enough, he worked a stint as an investment analyst embedded in France's Burgundian wine culture. Wine experiences abroad prepared him for another adventure, to move back across the Atlantic with his American-born wife, Peggy, and his two sons, and explore the possibility of opening his own winery.

Although this book is no complete autobiography, it does include snippets that give us insight into the unlikely immigration of the Duffelers in 1983 to a rundown, 320-acre farm on a peninsula between Colonial Williamsburg and the James River. Their efforts to tame this New World plot and begin to create a wine estate are the stuff of family legend.

Jump forward to today and a lot has changed. From a humble start has come a large, modern wine estate, more than 50 acres of vineyards, an Old World-inspired hotel, dining facilities and expansive accommodations for day visitors who come for special events or simply to sample wines. Sadly, Peggy, who worked so hard alongside Patrick to make the winery dream come true, died in 2004 after a long illness. It has fallen to Françoise, who worked in France in the hospitality industry and to whom Patrick was wed in 2007, to be hostess of the estate, and contributor as interior decorator.

I find it interesting to read this book from a yin and yang perspective. For example, a car enthusiast involved with Formula One racing becomes a wine producer and hotelier. The two pursuits may seem very different, yet both involve a heady blend of risk and exhilaration. Patrick is upfront about his appreciation of Old World tradition in winemaking, yet also defends modern New World techniques and equipment the Williamsburg Winery sometimes employs. I found fascinating his description of state-of-the-art wine filtration systems, but I was interested even more in the winery's use of egg-shaped concrete fermentation tanks that hold 188 gallons and are based on 5,000-year-old designs.

Then there is the yin and yang of the wines themselves. On one hand are the everyday, "grocery store" wines such as Governor's White, a crowd-pleasing, off-dry wine of modest price. On the other end of the Williamsburg Winery spectrum are super premium, "splurge" wines. The mix of the two keep the winery on solid financial footing.

The later wines include my favorite, Trianon red, which is anchored by cabernet franc, and the top-of-the-line Adagio red, a blend of the best Bordeaux varieties that are available in a given year. Adagio, by the way, as well as the winery's Acte 12 Chardonnay, have won the prestigious Governor's Cup honoring Virginia's best wines.

When Patrick sent me an early manuscript for this book, he made it clear that one of his goals was to give due credit in these pages to the winemaking, hospitality, marketing and business people who have contributed to the success of the Williamsburg Winery and its satellite establishments. A section of the book written by professional writers is composed of tributes to these people, and I want to mention one: Matthew Meyer, the longtime chief winemaker. He has a well-deserved reputation for inspired innovation and has made significant contributions to a Virginia style of winemaking that niches the state's wines between the sweet-oak density of those from California and the understated elegance of those from the Old World.

But, in the end, when I think of the Williamsburg Winery I think of Patrick Duffeler, and of the tour de force he mounted to make it a reality.

James Raper, Humble Steward wine columnist
Coastal Virginia, January 2021

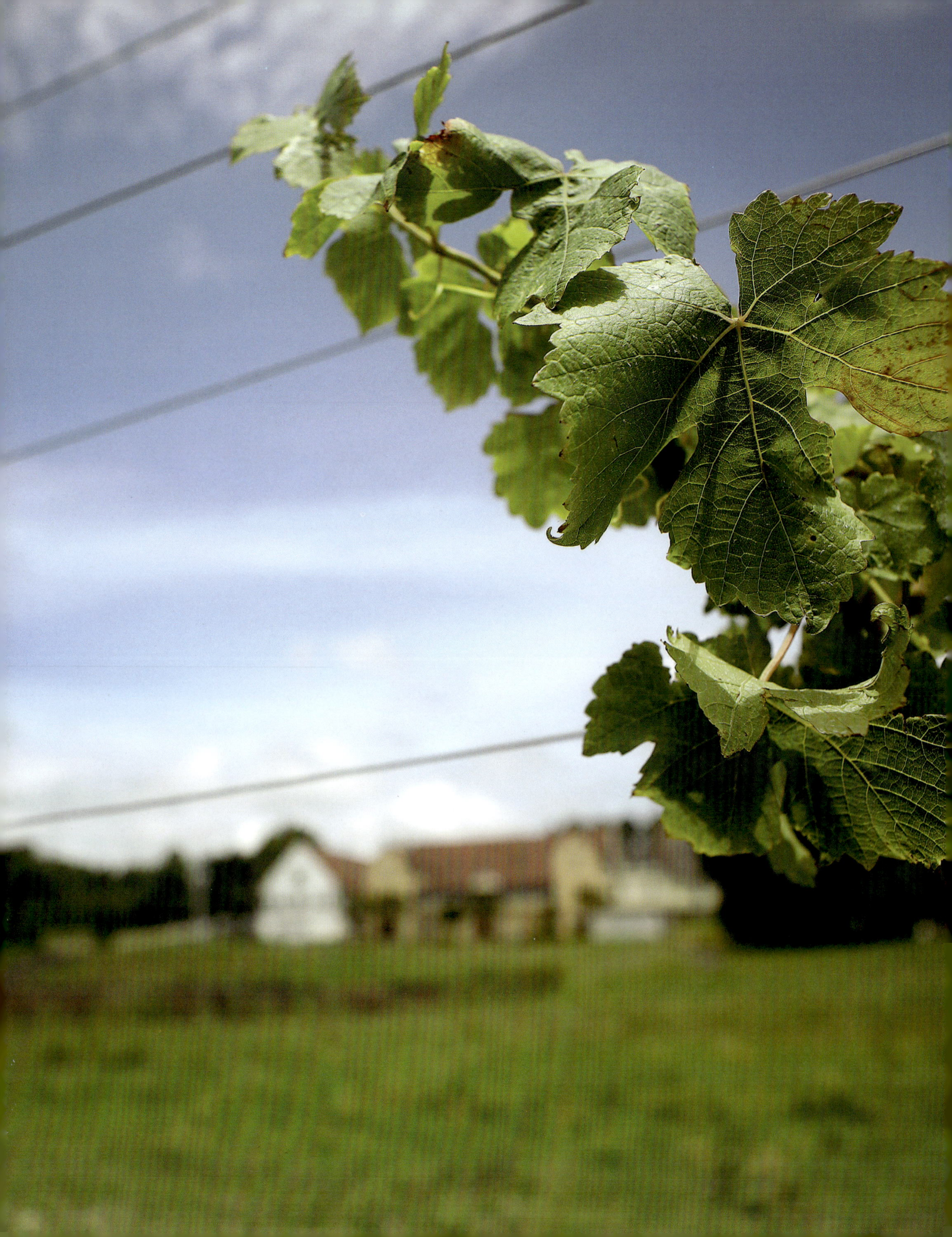

Part 1

– The Art and Science of Viticulture at the Williamsburg Winery

– The Art and Science of Winemaking at the Williamsburg Winery

– Barrels, Bottles and Corks

– Advanced Technologies in Winemaking

– A Listing of Regions, Wine Styles and Major Grape Varietals

– Wine Aromas and Compounds

– A Marriage of Wine and Food

Vines as they arrive in April ready for planting.

THE ART & SCIENCE OF VITICULTURE
at the Williamsburg Winery

The making of fine wines starts in the vineyards.

Vineyards are located throughout the world, from the Georgian and Moldavian republics on the Black Sea to the Pacific island of New Zealand, from the banks of the Rhine River in Germany to the Maipo Valley in Chile.

Different vines are suited to different climates, and over the years, in Europe, especially, tradition has emphasized varietals that seem best suited for specific microclimates.

Vines and Varietals

There are several basic classifications of grapevines:

- *Vitis vinifera,* the traditional wine grapes of Europe, including such well-known varieties as Chardonnay, Cabernet Sauvignon, Cabernet Franc, Merlot, and Riesling
- Native American varietals, such as the Concord and the Scuppernong
- Hybrids, or crosses, including the French American varietals Vidal Blanc and Seyval Blanc, and the German hybrid Müller-Thürgau

Rootstock

Grapes can be grown on their rootstock or grafted onto the rootstock of another species. In the 19th century, Europe's vineyards were nearly obliterated when the plague of phylloxera was accidentally transported from America. Today vinifera vines are grafted onto indigenous American rootstocks, which over time, have become adapted to native pests, including phylloxera and environmental conditions.

The rootstock gives rise to the plant's root system, which absorbs both moisture and nutrients from the soil. Rootstocks cultivated for grafting purposes bear unromantic names like AxR-1, 3309C, and SO4. They differ in such fundamental characteristics as vigor, hardiness, and suitability to specific soils and climatic conditions. The careful selection of the right rootstock for a particular variety of grape and the location of the vineyard are critically important factors in viticulture.

Clones

A given varietal of wine grape may have one or more clones. A clone is a variety within a variety. Some clones may favor higher yield, while others are selected for their special flavors. The proper matching of a varietal clone to the rootstock and the vineyard location is essential to successful winemaking and the overall health and longevity of the vine.

Soil and Topography

Grapes tend to be selective about the ground in which they are planted. Before a site is chosen, a thorough analysis must be made to ensure that it has the right mineral content, good drainage capacity, and the proper degree of soil compaction. Although most often planted on gently sloping or hilly terrain, vineyards can also thrive on flat ground as long as there is sufficient drainage. One of the best fertilizers for a vineyard is pomace—the skins, pits, and stems left over from crush—which is composted, mixed with mulch, and spread between the rows.

The orientation of the rows can vary, and the density of the plants per acre may range from around 600-800 per acre in most American vineyards to 4,000 vines per acre in Burgundy. In France, viticulture is highly regulated because of its importance as a major industry and a source of great national pride. Most French viticulture standards were established in the 19th century. French winegrowers today are actively seeking to modernize these standards to incorporate the findings of ongoing research.

To grow quality grapes a compromise has to be reached between yield per plant (the pounds of grapes that can be harvested), the canopy (the total surface of leaves developed during the summer by each plant), the need to avoid potential diseases, and the vitality of the vine itself.

Sun, Rain, and Canopy

Healthy berries with the proper balance of sugars, acids, and varietal flavors are the result of the right balance of sun, rain, canopy, and soil constituents. While nature plays a major role in determining the quality of the vintage, the viticulturist also can significantly affect the outcome of the growing season through proper vineyard management.

A vine's canopy is the cover of leaves that it develops each summer. Within the leaves, photosynthesis occurs when sunshine converts carbon dioxide, water, and inorganic salts into carbohydrates, and the grapes themselves are the primary beneficiaries of this process. Without enough sunlight, however, the clusters will not ripen sufficiently, reducing the Brix, or sugar, levels in the grapes. Strategic leaf pulling, which opens up the canopy to expose the clusters to more sunlight, enhances the development of both sugars and flavors in the grapes. Canopy management in concert with soil management are key to producing quality grapes.

Without rain, there would be no vine, no grapes, no juice, and no wine. But too much rain will dilute the sugars and flavors in the fruit and produce unexciting wines. Not enough rain will shrivel the grapes. A lack of rain can be compensated for by drip irrigation, which releases a small amount of water at the base of the plants, thus minimizing evaporation and conserving water. Grapevines are hardy and, in some cases, will develop roots that go as deep as forty feet. The roots take moisture and nutrients from the soil to develop the plant itself (new shoots in the spring) and the grape clusters. Too many clusters will not only weaken the plant but also affect the quality of the berries. Crop thinning in the early stages of cluster development will ensure a much higher grade of fruit at the time of harvest.

Controlling Disease and Pests

Sprays and mechanical means are used to control weeds in the vineyard. Sprays are also used to control fungi and other disease organisms, which can damage or destroy the grapes or the vines. Considerable research has gone into developing preventive and curative agents that are not harmful to the environment. Sprays are carefully monitored by the Department of Agriculture to ensure appropriate application.

Not all the diseases affect grapevines; phylloxera has been the most publicized. Not only did it threaten the entire winegrowing world in the 19th century, a hundred years later, it has also caused significant damage in California. Phylloxera is an infinitesimally small insect that attacks the vine's root system in great swarms, depriving the plant of nutrition and ultimately killing it. Vinifera (European) varieties of grapes are especially vulnerable. The most effective prevention for this scourge has been the grafting of vines onto naturally resistant, namely, native American rootstock. Over the years, phylloxera has mutated, and many growers, having grafted their vinifera varieties onto rootstock that was resistant to earlier forms of the insect, had become complacent in the belief that the threat of phylloxera had been eradicated.

There are numerous other diseases, both bacterial and viral, that affect grapevines. Some can be effectively controlled, some not. Current research is focused on environmentally friendly remedies and genetic engineering to create more disease-resistant vines.

Trellising

Trellising is another of many variables to be considered by the viticulturist. Traditionally vines were free-standing. They were head pushed (pruned back to the main trunk) in the winter and allowed to redevelop in the spring without the aid of a stake. The trellis is the combination of posts and wires used by modern vineyardists to manage the growth of the vines. Trellising allows the vine to unleash its vigor. A trellis system consists of a stake for each plant, posts positioned at every third or fourth vine, and a series of wires stretched between the posts to support the weight of the fruit and anchor the shoots so as to minimize wind damage. There are many different types of trellising.

The Williamsburg Winery favors the vertical system, which encourages the shoots to grow upward, allowing the sun to shine directly on the berries, a factor vital to the development of aroma compounds and overall quality. Other vineyards have adopted alternative types of trellising. The lyre, or U trellis, allows a single plant to develop two vertical canopies side by side. The Geneva double curtain is similar to the U concept but in reverse. With the GDC system, the fruit is concentrated on the top, and the canopy falls downward.

During the winter, many man-hours are spent pruning the vines to limit the number of buds and reduce the yield in order to enhance fruit quality. In the spring, as the canopy develops, shoots are thinned by hedging the rows. Leaf pulling takes place to ensure good air circulation and sufficient sun exposure on the berries.

Netting

For many birds as well as virtually all wildlife (deer, raccoons, turkeys, geese, and opossums all love ripe grapes) wine grapes appear to be the ultimate delicacy, and it's not unheard of for entire crops to be lost in a few days to an opportunistic convention of these freeloading animals connoisseurs. In Williamsburg, already in the early spring, the vines need to be protected from predatory herbivores that love tender vine buds. To protect the vines from pilferage during the summer, netting is draped over the rows as soon as the berries begin to ripen and left on until the grapes are harvested.

Microclimate

Regardless of how closely and consistently a winegrower may adhere to the best practices of modern viticulture, and with all other things being equal, it is still a truism in the world of winemaking that no two vineyards will produce the same wine. From vintage to vintage, the microclimate in which the grapes are grown imparts its unique characteristics to each year's wine. At the Williamsburg Winery, we are proud to point out that wine is one of the last unstandardized products available to the consumer. Every vineyard is unique, every season is original, and every wine is one of a kind.

Harvest

At the Williamsburg Winery, harvest begins in late August or early September and lasts until mid-October. As the time for grape picking approaches, the viticulturist and the winemaker must decide between them which characteristics they want to optimize in the grapes of a particular variety or from a particular vineyard—whether to harvest for sugar, for acid, or for specific aroma compounds. Their decision will be influenced by the overall growing season and the styles of wine the winemaker has in mind and will determine precisely when the harvest is made.

Weather conditions during the last six weeks prior to harvest will have an enormous impact on the ultimate quality of the fruit and the decisions reached by the winemaker and the viticulturist. One always hopes for plenty of sunshine and little or no rain in the period just before harvest so that the fruit can reach full maturity, and the juices will remain concentrated with the sugars and flavors. No sprays are applied during the last two weeks to eliminate the potential of any residue remaining on the grapes. Harvest should be done in the early hours of the morning, or at night, to prevent the grapes from being damaged in the sun. Temperatures at harvest can sometimes reach 90°F, and white grapes (which mature first) are best fermented at around 55°F to protect the delicate flavors.

Viticulture Research

Enormous improvements have been made to the art and science of viticulture and winemaking in recent decades. California, Australia, Italy, and all major wine regions have demonstrated leadership oriented to the requirements of their areas. Virginia has its own state-funded vineyard research station and a group of dedicated scientists to assist in managing the growth of viticulture in the Commonwealth. Considerable research is still needed to identify and define the specific characteristics of Virginia's many and varied microclimates and multiple soils that may or may not make them suitable for grape growing. Virginia Tech has undertaken numerous studies at its research station in Winchester, focusing its efforts on varietal research, soil, and microclimate suitability standards, pruning standards, and disease control.

The Williamsburg Winery has, for some time, formulated its standards that reflect its unique viticultural environment.

Virginia experiences less variation in its annual weather patterns than France, but more than California. With less sunshine intensity, our state's wines do not have the massive fruit-forward, blockbuster flavors typical of certain California wines. Virginia wines exhibit more of the subtleties and complexities characteristic of European wines. Virginia has begun experimenting and successfully so with making bigger wines, particularly with the introduction of the Petit Verdot and Tannat varietals.

Actually, the recent trends have favored the Virginia style of wines. Top California vintners have focused on more subtle flavor, inspired by the classic elegant French wines. The nose (the entire bouquet of aromas), the palate, and the aftertaste in the best of these wines will show consistency in their flavor and aroma compounds. The Williamsburg Winery's varietal wines are designed to be enjoyed after they have aged a while in the bottle: *Acte 12 Chardonnay,* for example, for one or two years; *Gabriel Archer Reserve* for five to ten years and *Adagio* for eight to twenty years.

Eli Ramos, our senior Viticulturist dumps grapes in the bin.

Pruning (1) in January and February helps balance the vine growth and the number of grape clusters to ensure healthy vines.

Planting New Vines (2) takes place in early spring.

Training & Tying (3) in the spring consists of attaching vines to wires that will help bear the weight of the fruit and spread out the foliage for maximum exposure to sunlight and breezes.

Fertilizing (4) annually in the spring ensures proper plant nutrient balance.

Mowing & Weeding (5) encourages healthier fruit production by reducing competition from weeds and grass.

Cluster Thinning & Shoot Thinning (6) in the early summer promotes quality and ensures that the vines are not stressed

Pest & Disease Control (7) in the early summer consists of regular and careful application of selected sprays to avoid plant and fruit damage from rot, disease, and insects.

Fruit Development (8) during the summer relies on a good balance between rain and sunshine, particularly during the last six weeks of the growing season. At the Williamsburg Winery, irrigation is accomplished by the drip method. Sugar and acid levels are monitored weekly.

Harvest (9) usually begins in late August and ends in October.

Four of the red fermenters.

THE ART & SCIENCE OF WINEMAKING
at the Williamsburg Winery

Harvest or crush begins around late August or early September. Each varietal has a different schedule. Grapes ready for picking early include Vidal. Then come Chardonnay, Viognier, and other white grapes. Red grapes, such as Cabernet Franc, Merlot, and Cabernet Sauvignon, Petit Verdot, and Tannat, are harvested from late September through mid-October.

The best grapes deserve special attention. It is important to pick the fruit when it is at the peak of ripeness but not let it deteriorate. Not unlike fresh fruit at the supermarket, the hard fruit travels well but does not exhibit the fully developed flavors of ripe fruit. While most quality-oriented smaller operations continue to harvest by hand, the relative speed of mechanical harvesting allows the large producers to gather the fruit at the right moment and transport it to the winery in a timely manner. In Virginia, the daytime temperature at harvest may vary from as much as 90°F in early September to a cool 55-60°F in October, virtually the reverse of the desired fermentation temperatures for white grapes and red grapes. Because the fermentation process is fundamentally different for white and red grapes, each type is handled in special fermentation tanks.

At the winery, the white grapes are pumped into a stemmer/crusher, which separates the stems from the grapes and gently crushes the berries to allow the juice to flow from what is defined as a must (the pulp, juice, and skins of the crushed grapes). After the press, the juice is then fermented either in barrels, in eggs, or in stainless steel tanks. When ready, it is filtered and bottled.

Grapes for red wines are fermented with the skins, which provide the color at a temperature of approximately 85°F and then pressed and barreled in oak for aging of up to twelve or eighteen months.

The fundamental taste of a wine depends on the grape variety and conditions affecting the fruit in the vineyard. Its style expresses the combination of winemaking techniques employed by the winemaker, with the recommendations of the winery's tasting panel. Rigorous analysis and scientific controls are applied at every step to observe and guide the evolution of the wine in order to achieve the highest quality standards possible. When the winemaker determines that the wine is ready to be bottled, the bottles are cleaned, filled, vacuum corked, capped, and labeled on an automated bottling line. They are then placed in shipping cartons and aged in a climate-controlled environment. After aging a while longer in the customer's care, the finished product is ready to be enjoyed.

The juice runs from the press.

Matthew Meyer, Winemaker, pushes a bin on the rollers to the scale, ready for dumping into the auger.

The drawing above features an old press seen in Alsace, France, which could handle as much as a ton of grapes. The seventeenth century press was almost 7 feet tall.

Our stainless-steel press. The bladder inside the drum is controlled by a computer to balance the pressure determined by the winemaker, and has a capacity of pressing up to 14 tons of grapes.

The cluster of grapes falling into the hopper and going into the auger.

The juice is falling into large stainless-steel trays and then pumped into the large tanks, as shown on page 42.

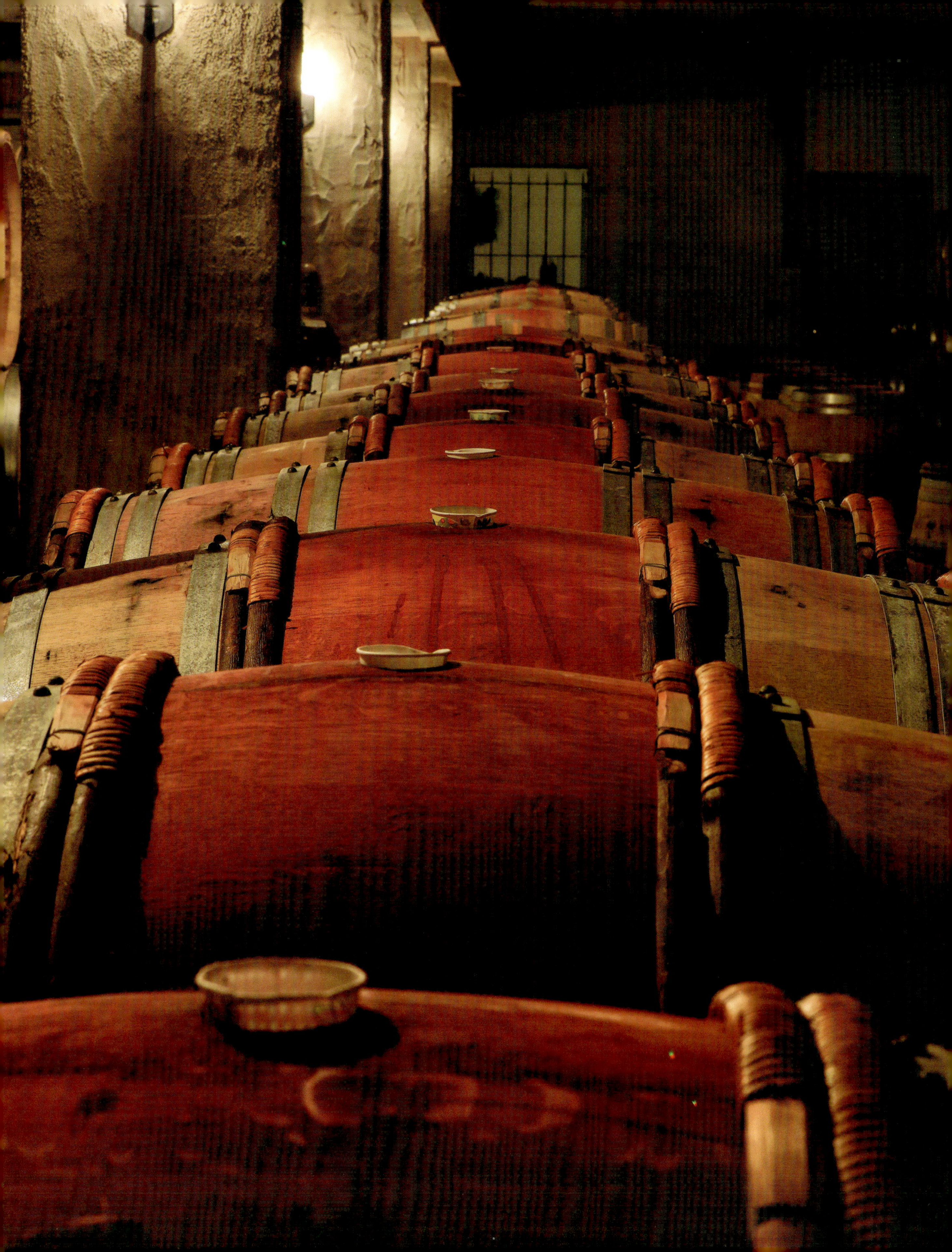

BARRELS, BOTTLES, AND CORKS

Barrels

The art of barrel making is a subject steeped in history, a craft reflecting centuries of accumulated know-how. The life of a barrel—from its conception to finished products, from its use in the cellar to its eventual decay—is a story in itself. It involves artisans and craftsmen, those working in the majestic oak forests, as well as those who assemble the finished vessel.

Oak has been the wood of choice for barrel making for centuries. Oakwood is robust, hard, and dense, which gives it strength. The common oak in France (Quercus Pedunculata) is also widely grown throughout the rest of Europe. It has a relatively wide grain and, as a result, releases its tannins fairly quickly. This tree grows rapidly and is found mainly in south-central France in the former province of Limousin, a region that also gave the name to the "limousine" vehicles—large horse-drawn carriages with a hood to protect the driver.

The robur oak (Quercus Sessiflora) exhibits much slower growth. Its wood is finer-grained, softer, and less dense. This variety is regarded as having the mildest tannins, which gives up more slowly during the fermenting and aging of wine, making it more valued as a source of barrel wood. It is harvested primarily from the Tronçais Forest in France. Allier and Nevers are two densely forested regions in central France, which are also well known for producing oak used in barrel making.

Oak from other regions of the world, including central Europe, Hungary, Bulgaria, Romania, and the Caucasus, is also used to make wine barrels. The American white oak has been used for many decades for nurturing whiskeys, bourbon, and sour mash. It is now used in French-style barrel-making in the United States. Virginia oak has been identified as having a particularly favorable characteristic for wine-barrel making, specifically, a relatively tight grain. Kentucky, Indiana, and Pennsylvania are other states where oak barrels are sourced.

The oak trees that are selected for barrel making have a diameter of from one and a half to two feet. In France, that means a tree over 100 years old. After being cut down, the tree is timbered into cask wood. French oak will be split, as opposed to sawed. To make quality staves, the wood must have a straight grain, its fibers must be parallel, and it must be free of knots and splinters. Before they can be used, the staves must be air-dried for two to three years. A newly felled tree contains up to 80% water. To be ready for barrel making a stave's humidity must be reduced to below 20%, preferably 15%. Interestingly, in order for the wood to dry satisfactorily, it must be stacked with spacers and left in the open air—exposed to the rain, wind, cold, and heat. The wood works through this curing process until it achieves structural stability or integrity, which makes it resistant to contracting and expanding.

When the rough planks are ready, they are turned into finished staves by a craftsman known as a skiver, so-called after the tool he uses—a skive (also called a whitening knife). The specialist responsible for actually assembling the barrel is the hooper, who is assigned by the fitter who works the metallic parts. Barrel making is a handcraft demanding much skill and expenditure of time. The different stages are, briefly, as follows:

- Shortening and trimming the staves to exact dimensions
- Finishing the staves, including paring, scraping the insides, arrowing and jointing so they will fit snugly when drawn together and secured in place by the hoops
- Assembling the barrel

The assembly starts with the bung stave (which is slightly wider than the others and has been drilled with the bunghole for filling and emptying the barrel). The staves are arranged upright in a metal collar called the molding hoop, forming a cone, and then placed over a fire fueled by oak scraps. As the staves heat up and become supple, a cable is tightened around them, and they are drawn together. The cable is then replaced by a permanent barrel hoop. The rest of the hoops are put into position, further tightening the staves, and the cooper turns his attention to the task of singeing, or "toasting," the inside of the barrel. The level of toast will have a major impact on the way the barrel influences the wine. Depending on the objectives of the winemaker, barrels with light, medium, or heavy toast may be selected. After the barrel has been toasted, the heads, or bottoms, are installed, using a hammer to drive them into place from inside the barrel and a "head puller" to set the other in place from the outside.

The quality of the barrels is of paramount importance if the winemaker is to achieve the high standards required of reserve wines. While the wine is in the barrels, an exchange of wood, wine, and atmosphere occurs as follows: A light aspiration takes place through the pores of the wood, and the wine acquires tanning (natural preservatives) and aroma compounds from the oak while being impacted by a very light oxidation. All these factors combine to change the aroma and flavor structure of barrel-aged wines, which require careful monitoring, including the regular "topping off" of each cask to ensure that it remains full to the bottom of the bung.

Standard oak barrels contain 60 gallons or 300 bottles. Oversized barrels, known as puncheons, will hold as much as 120 gallons, or 600 bottles. Large vats of 1,000 to 3,000 gallons used to be quite common for the fermentation of red wines. They have been replaced by stainless steel tanks, which provide the ideal vessel for a temperature-controlled fermentation prior to barrel aging. In Italy, the barrel aging is done in large units and held for two or three years.

The art of barrel making is in many respects unchanged in many of the smaller barrel-making companies. The drawing above represents a barrel maker inspired from a picture in the 1753 Encyclopedia of Diderot France.

Bottles

The early history of bottle making in the Western world is obscure. Hugh Johnson, the author of *The Encyclopedia of Wine* (one of the best books ever written on the subject), refers to discoveries on the shores of the Black Sea of wine container dating as far back as 3000 B.C. Amphoras were commonly used by the Greeks and Romans. They were made of clay, kiln-fired, and could be sealed. In 1970, I saw a team of French archaeologists bring amphoras up from the bottom of the port of Antibes, where the scientists were researching the remains of a Greek vessel that had sunk in that harbor some 2,500 years ago. The amphoras were still sealed and still contained wine, which obviously was well beyond its time.

The use of bottles as a means of conserving wine is, on the other hand, relatively recent.

Glass production is a fire craft, alongside metallurgy. The base materials needed for the manufacture of glass are sand and alkali. Archaeologists tell us that the glassmaking began sometime between 1000 and 3000 B.C. on the shores of ancient Phoenicia. The craft was introduced into northern Europe by the Romans. There were glassmaking furnaces all over medieval Europe, including England, by the 13th century.

GLASSMAKING AT JAMESTOWN

The drawing was inspired by visiting glassmaking in Jamestown in 1990 when they were demonstrating 17th-century glassmaking as practiced in Jamestown Island.

Production of the "green" glass bottle did not occur until the closing years of the 16th century. Great strides were made in the following century in the craft of bottle manufacturing. Venice became renowned for its glassmaking factories. To this day, multicolored and layered Venetian glass is an art form to be admired in the houses that line the back canals of the famous Italian seaport.

The earliest wine bottles were blown, as opposed to being molded. While molded bottles are as old as antiquity, mechanical molding developed only in the early 19th century, and with the consequence that the craft and industry of glass blowing drew to a close. It survives today only as an art form.

The shapes of wine bottles have evolved over time, and the designs are quite specific to certain periods, making the dating of antique specimens fairly easy. **Figure A** shows a shaft and globe bottle, a shape prominent in 1650. By 1680, bottles had become squatter and were defined as onion-shaped **(Figure B)**. By 1690, the onion bottle had become a "squat onion" **(Figure C).** 1710 saw the introduction of the bladder bottle, also known as the "tavern bottle" **(Figure D).** Its shape gave it much needed stability on the tables of inns and taverns, whose patrons often became quite rowdy in their enjoyment of the wine.

By 1730, the bottle had taken the shape of a wooden mallet (**Figure E**). Toward the latter part of the 18th century, bottles were beginning to look more like the modern containers used today. Specialty bottles were created, such as the square and the octagonal bottle. Decanters with a pouring neck were developed, and forms followed the fancy of the artist in creating regional styles as well as varying sizes.

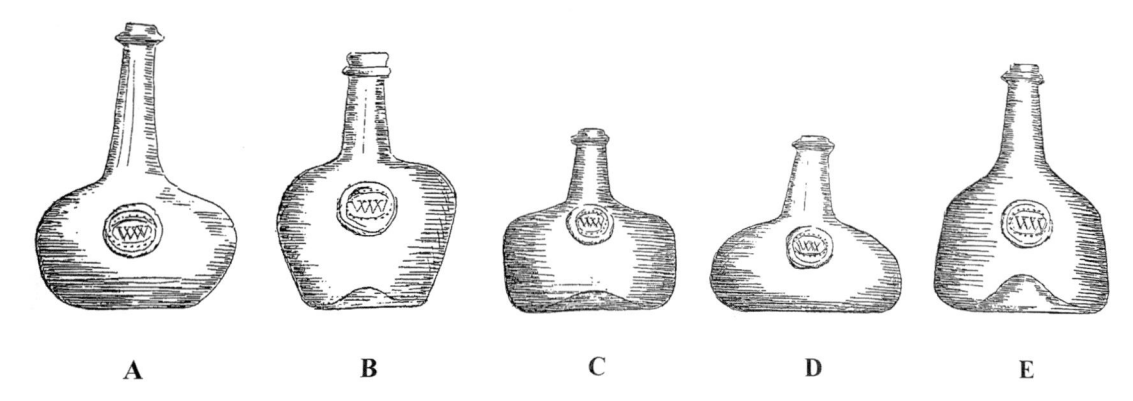

The evolution of glass bottle shapes.

Throughout much of its history, the bottle making, like most industries, has not escaped becoming the object—some would argue the target—of legislation and regulation. In England, the production of glass, including bottles, was taxed under Oliver Cromwell in 1645. Before that, in 1636, a law had been enacted, which restricted the sale of wine by the bottle. It was an early attempt at consumer protection, aimed at regulating the measure of wine received by the customer. Since no two bottles could be blown exactly alike, the volume could vary considerably from bottle to bottle.

An individual might purchase a cask of his favorite Bordeaux wine and have it shipped to a London trader, who would act as his agent and also undertake to bottle the wine for the client. The customer might send the merchant some 300 empty bottles for this purpose, but the bottles that he got back were, in all likelihood, not the ones he himself had supplied. In these transactions, the casks themselves remained with the merchants, and people worried that they might not be getting the full contents of their barrels.

The law was a reaction to the excessive petty litigation that clogged the royal courts as a result. It required that, in order for wine to be bottled by the merchant, seals had to be affixed to the bottles that would clearly identify the owners. The act had a profound effect in that it led to an immediate increase in the use of private wine bottles. In England, individual consumers ordered hundreds of bottles every year, and bottles exhibiting the seals of their owners came to English America as well, while bottles from customers in continental Europe continued to show none. Today, virtually all bottles of port wine bear such seals, and the royal act survives as a tradition in a trade still dominated almost entirely by English merchants.

Color in glass results when specific minerals—metallic oxides—are introduced into the mix. There are three tints which have prevailed in the wine world:

- Champagne green (actually dark green), found in all viticultural areas
- Dead leaf green, a lighter green traditional in the Burgundy and the Rhone regions of France
- Amber, a brown tint commonly used in Italy and in the Rheingau of Germany.

The shapes of wine bottles in the 19th century became recognized as representative of their region of production. There are four classic styles, each associated with specific winegrowing areas. In the illustration below, they are, from left to right:

- The Burgundy bottle, also used in the Rhone Valley of France, in Spain for Riojas, and red wines in the French-speaking region of Switzerland
- The Bordeaux bottle, also used in the Chianti area, as well as other Italian wine-producing regions, and in the Ticino province of Switzerland
- The German bottle is known as Hock, which is restricted by regulation to brown for the Rheingau and green for the Mosel region
- The flattened saddlebag bottle (known in German as the "Bocksbeutel"), again regulated in Germany, where it is reserved exclusively for wines from the Franconia area. This bottle has been well known in the United States as the container of inexpensive Portuguese wines

Modern wine bottle shapes.

Bottle Closures, Corks, Capsules, and Screwcaps

How to keep the wine from going bad was a problem that faced the very first winemaker and has challenged his successors ever since. Air is the number one enemy of wine because it carries organisms that can degrade the wine, even turn it into vinegar, in very short order. Natural cork has proven to be remarkably suited to the task of providing an airtight stopper for wine bottles.

In earlier times, wines were often kept in the barrels for decades. Filled to the bung, the casks were regularly topped off to allow for the mild evaporation that takes place through the pores of the oak. Today, extended aging usually takes place in the bottle, more often than not in the consumer's own cellar. It has long been recognized that in order for a wine to develop to its full potential in the bottle, the quality and integrity of the bottle's closure must be assured.

When glass wine bottles first came into use, they were hand blown. Care was taken to properly stop the bottles, but each neck had a slightly different shape. A cork was inserted into the neck and then covered with cloth and wax to ensure a good seal. With the introduction of molded bottles, neck sizes could be standardized in production, allowing the use of equally standardized corks. In the last century, the French took the initiative of defining national standards for the necks of bottles and their specific interior designs, doing away with regional standards, which in some instances required corks of 22, 23, 24, or 25 mm diameters for bottles of the same volume.

Natural corks are cut from the bark of a specific variety of oak grown in the Mediterranean area. Most natural corks come from Portugal. The tissue of the bark is comprised of dead cells and air with a lower carbon dioxide content than atmospheric air. Cork is remarkable in that it is virtually impermeable to liquids, yet it will allow a gas to pass through very slowly. While it is basically water-resistant, it had an inherent humidity, varying anywhere from 3% to 15%.

A cork's elasticity depends to a certain degree on ambient humidity and temperature, as well as its cellulose structure. After compression, a natural cork returns to almost 85% of its original size instantaneously. Within twenty-four hours, it regains 98% of its original volume.

The quality of corks can vary greatly. In the early 1990s, with the demand for top-grade bottle closures increasing, the wine industry faced a shortage of cork caused by a rise in the incidence of infectious disease affecting the bark of the source trees. Consumers, restaurants, and wine competition judges alike experienced an abnormally high percentage of wines that had been "corked"—tainted with the unpleasant flavor imbued by a bad cork.

Partly in reaction to the shortage of natural cork and partly for purely economic reasons, a great many wine producers began using plastic corks. Despite efforts by the synthetic cork industry to imitate the cell structure of real cork, the structural integrity of some artificial corks has been brought into question. Certain wine producers who experimented for a while with plastic corks had gone back to using the real thing. The unique characteristics of natural cork are appreciated by the dedicated and experienced winemaker, who recognizes that the cork is critically important to the preservation and evolution of wine in the bottle.

The key question related to the use of synthetic corks vs. natural corks is the question of wines being sold for immediate consumption vs. wines being purchased for storage in a wine cellar where the subject temperature is approximately 60 degrees Fahrenheit.

The quality of synthetic corks has improved tremendously compared to some of the various composite corks that had appeared in the eighties and nineties.

It is about that time that Australian wine producers introduced the screwcap on the U.S. market for their popular brands. Australia's high-quality wines did stick to natural corks.

For wines that are designed for sale to consumers who will enjoy the wine within what market studies have indicated to be within forty-eight hours after purchase, the screwtaps are a practical and efficient method of closure.

The Williamsburg Winery has determined that with the 2020 vintage, its most popular wines will use screwcap closures.

Pressing the grapes. Details from a Renaissance wood carving.

Wessex Hundred
The
WILLIAMSBURG
WINERY LIMITED
WW
2018
PETIT VERDOT
Virginia
PRODUCED AND BOTTLED BY THE WILLIAMSBURG WINERY

Winemaker Matthew Meyer in front of some of our large stainless-steel tanks in Fermentation Room 1. Tanks in Fermentation Room 2 are even larger. In Fermentation Room 3, we incorporated tanks that were previously used in the Dominion Wine Cellar.

ADVANCED TECHNOLOGIES AND WINEMAKING

There are thousands of wineries in France, Italy, Germany, the United States, and many other countries all over the world. Wineries, while very collegial, compete in the marketplace, and it is this competitiveness that drives them to constantly search for ways to make better wines.

In many respects, winemaking can be compared to cooking. There are so many variables involved that the winemaker is faced with countless options when trying to decide which direction to take on the making of any given wine. Winemakers have unusually sensitive palates and seem to possess a sixth sense about how a particular wine will evolve. Just by tasting the unfermented juice at the time of crush, they can predict how the wine will taste after years of aging in the bottle. Yeast selection can have a dramatic impact on a wine's flavor. Besides being the living agents that convert sugar into alcohol, the yeast cells release chemical compounds during fermentation that evoke different flavors and aromas in the wine. Known as glycosides, these compounds are the catalysts of flavor development in wine. Experienced winemakers know precisely which strain of yeast to use in order to optimize the flavor potential of a particular wine.

The heart and soul of wine are its flavors. A great deal of wine research is currently focused on flavor and aroma enhancement. A grape's flavor package accurately reflects its *terroir*, a French word which in winemaking terms includes a vineyard's microclimatology as well as characteristics of the soil.

The impact of barrel aging on the flavor question is extremely important, and so is filtration. Excessive filtration, while delivering a totally clear wine entirely free of sediments, may strip it of some of its flavors. Recently, certain high-priced wines have been promoted as "unfiltered." These may exhibit richer flavors but will also show particulates, notably tartaric acid crystals, floating in the wine.

Wines are, by nature, very complex in their aromatic structures. There may be as many as 700 flavor components in the makeup of a single wine! With age, these will compound, blend, evolve, and change the character and taste of the wine. Consumers enjoy the range of flavors and flavor intensities to be experienced in different wines. A great deal of effort on the part of winemakers has been devoted to gaining a better understanding of the components in wine that contribute to this enjoyment.

As the age-old craft of winemaking continues to evolve in the modern setting, a deeper respect and appreciation for the inherent formulation of wine operates alongside a recognition of the benefits to be derived from directing that evolution through the use of laboratory testing and scientific controls.

Current academic studies in Virginia are centered on evaluating thermal vinification (which involves manipulating the temperature during fermentation in order to achieve certain results), on flavor enhancement, and on the role of nitrogen in preserving wine quality. These studies hold great promise for the future of winemaking everywhere. While some winemakers consider themselves traditionalists and non-interventionists, others take a more proactive role, devoting a significant portion of their time to research and development inside their own wineries. For example, in an environment where American marketing campaigns have placed most of the emphasis on varietal wines, many winemakers are seeking to improve their expertise in the art of blending, a skill that is taken to its highest level in the Bordeaux region of France.

At the Williamsburg Winery, our approach to winemaking mirrors the character and identity of the establishment. Williamsburg produces wines that reflect a traditional approach. At the same time, science and modern technology are employed to assist in delivering to our customers a full range of wines—from simple, value-oriented labels for casual dining to highly structured, complex wines for more elegant occasions.

In Virginia, we are quite fortunate. Winemakers follow the traditional approach of the industry of exchanging notes about winemaking techniques, including experimentation. The Winemakers Research Exchange in Virginia is a great addition to this tradition. The California case of Kendall-Jackson where the firm sued an ex-winemaker for having carried with himself the pseudo winemaking techniques is very unusual in our industry.

The airlock, which is inserted in the corks of the barrel for wine in fermentation, allowing gas to be released and no air to enter.

Stacey is taking a sample from one of the tanks.

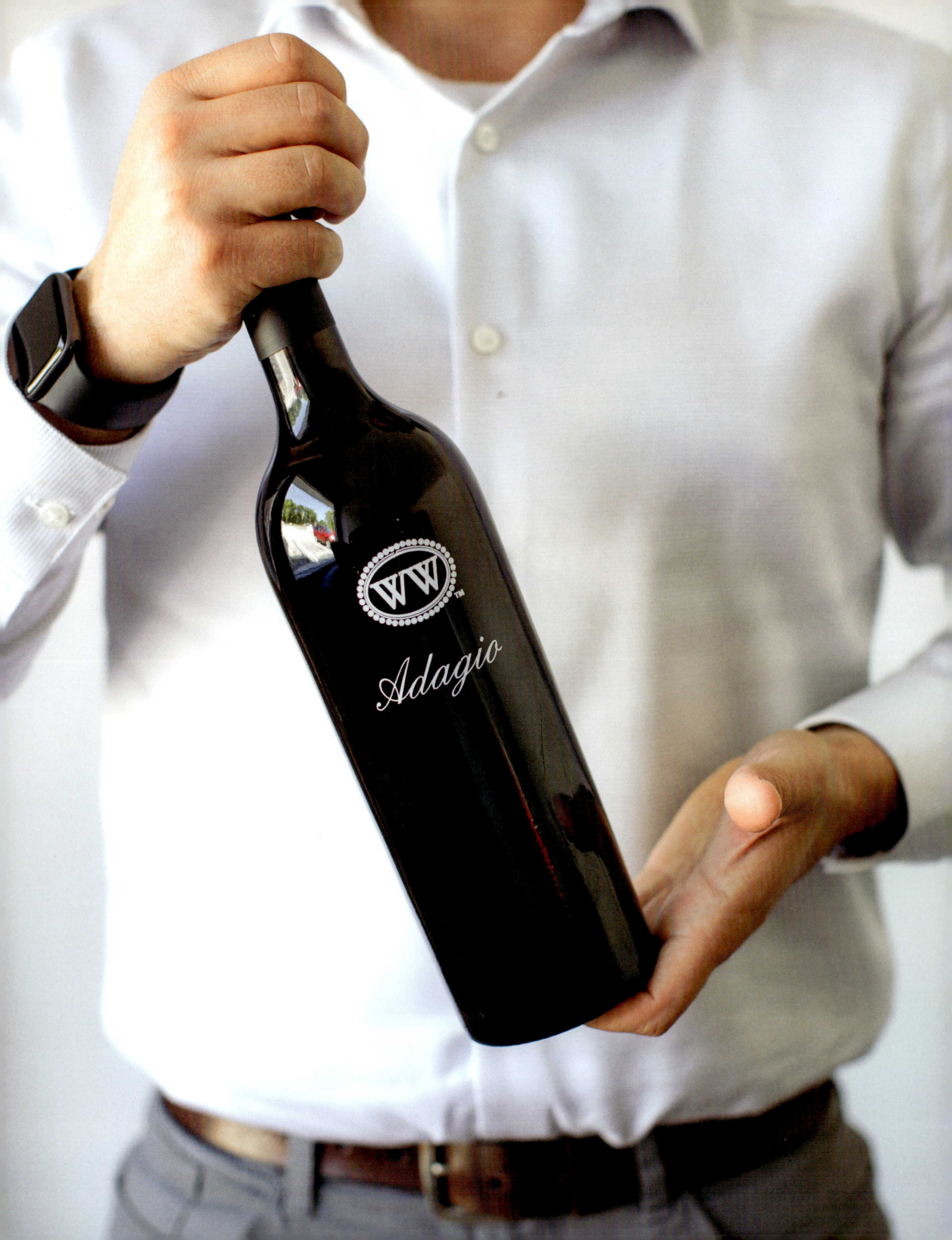
WW
Adagio

A LISTING OF REGIONS, WINE STYLES, & MAJOR GRAPE VARIETALS

REGIONS

Barolo. Produced using Nebbiolo grape from northern Italy's Piedmont region, Barolo is often referred to as the King of Wine. Full-bodied, complex, and featuring both high acidity and tannins, Barolo wines are perfect for pairing with food, including meat and pasta dishes.

Bordeaux. One of the most prestigious wine regions in the world, Bordeaux serves Cabernet Sauvignon and Merlot driven blends as well as sweet wines made from Sémillon, Sauvignon Blanc, and Muscadelle. The area is divided into three distinct regions: the Left Bank, Right Bank, and Entre-Deux-Mers.

Burgundy. A wine region in eastern France that serves some of the most sought after and expensive bottles in the world. Its reds are mostly made from Pinot Noir and its whites are made from Chardonnay.

Chianti. A world-famous Italian wine region located between the Tuscan provinces of Siena and Florence. Specializes in red wines made from Sangiovese grape.

Rioja. An iconic Spanish wine region, Rioja is known for producing age-worthy Tempranillo-driven red wines. White Rioja wines blend Malvasia and Viura with a handful of other white varietals.

Vino Nobile di Montepulciano. Named after the Tuscan town of Montepulciano, this red wine is predominantly made using Sangiovese grapes, which are known locally as Prugnolo. With gentle tannins and bright acidity, these wines pair wonderfully with a variety of foods.

WINE STYLES

Rosé Wine. Produced by soaking red grapes on their skins for shorter durations than red wines (no longer than two or three days), rosé wines range in color from pale salmon to deep pink. A summer staple and excellent food wine.

Sparkling Wines. Made by fermenting a still wine for a second time, sparkling wines are made in a range of sweetnesses, from extra-brut to demi-sec.

WHITE VARIETALS

Aligoté. A tart, grape of Burgundy. It is the ideal white wine to be used in making kir, the delightful aperitif concocted of white wine and crème de cassis.

Albariño or Alvarinho. A white grape grown in Galicia, Monção, and Melgaço, where it is used to make varietal white wines. Albariño is the Galician name for the grape; in Portugal it is known as Alvarinho, and sometimes as Cainho Branco.

Chardonnay. This wine in the New World is big, creamy, and juicy, with copious amounts of oak. In Burgundy, it is more complex and long-lived, with less tropical and more mineral and apple flavors, reflecting the cooler climate of the region. Chardonnay is an essential grape for *méthode champenoise*—style wines around the world.

Chenin Blanc. This grape is grown widely throughout the world (it is South Africa's most importantly variety) but rarely exhibits the character of the Loire Valley's great Vouvray and Savennieres. Here the wines are powerful, pungent, great, whether sweet or dry and amazingly long-lived. Twenty years or more is the norm for good vintages from the Loire.

French Colombard. Traditionally important in the Cognac region of France, it has given way to Ugni Blanc. Blended to less distinctive wines in the U.S. and South Africa.

Gewürztraminer. A friendly grape of the Muscat family, with a rich, pungent character. It is good in Germany and Italy; great in Alsace, where even when dry, it is so pungent it usually goes best with dessert.

Grüner Veltliner. Austria's signature white grape. Noted for its distinct herbal notes, Grüner Veltliner is an excellent accompaniment with hard to pair ingredients like white asparagus.

Malvasia. Perhaps the world's oldest grape, this rich and textured dessert wine, does great work in Greece, Spain, Italy, and Madeira. In Italy, it is often blended with Chianti in place of Trebbiano. Malvasia Nera, the red clone, also performs well as a dry wine in Apulia.

Marsanne. It is the more important of the two most widely planted white grapes of the northern Rhone (the other is Rouanne) because of its more consistent yields and more predictable vinification and maturation. Its flavors of rich orange and creamy lemon are allied with its waxy texture to create a unique experience. The grape is also grown in southern France and in the Côtes du Rhone.

Moscato. A sweet wine made using the Muscat grape. Most commonly associated with Moscato d' Asti, a slightly sparkling wine made in Italy's Piedmont region.

Müller-Thürgau. A pleasant and neutral grape of Germany and New Zealand that produces good wines.

Muscadelle. A grape with Muscat like aromas used to enrich and soften sweet (and sometimes dry) white Bordeaux. A small amount can bring something very pretty to the total wine.

Muscat. The finest selection of the Muscat family and a grape with several incarnations: Muscat Blanc à Petits Grains, or Muscat Frontignan; Brown Muscat; Muscat d' Alexandria; and Muscat Ottonel. Muscat à Petit Grains is the grape of southern French dessert wines (Muscat Beaumes de Venise), Italian wines (Goldenmuskateller), Italian sparklers (Moscato d' Asti and Asti Spumante), and even great Grecian wines (Samos).

Pinot Blanc. Identical to Pinot Gris in every way, except the Pinot Gris has sweet versions and proven greatness in Alsace. Instead, Pinot Blanc is merely delicious, with aromas of pear and a hint of stoniness in the best examples. A few bottlings emanate from Morey-Saint-Denis in Burgundy that are exciting and sometimes achieve greatness.

Pinot Grigio/Gris. Known as Pinot Grigio in Italy and Pinot Gris in France, this white grape serves refreshing, fruit-driven wines, with high acidity.

Riesling. One of the world's greatest grapes, Riesling, was treated with the respect it deserved 100 years ago when its finest bottlings routinely were bid for at higher prices than Lafite or Latour. Grown throughout the world with mixed results, America offers fine versions, and Australia produces the best New World vintages. Alsace offers the finest examples outside of Germany, with higher, more obstructive alcohol levels. All of Germany's great wines (except a tiny portion) are made from Riesling. This grape is rich and crisp when young but can age for ten to fifty years and beyond, depending upon the winemaking style.

Sauternes. Produced in the Graves region of Bordeaux, Sauternes is a lush dessert wine made with Sémillon, Sauvignon Blanc, and Muscadelle grapes. The presence of noble rot, a beneficial fungus, is crucial for the production of Sauternes Wines.

Sauvignon Blanc. This variety is blended with Sémillon to create dry white Bordeaux and is used in smaller portions for Sauternes and other French dessert wines. It is grown to the greatest effect in the Loire, especially in the Pouilly-Fumé and Sancerre appellations. Surprisingly, New Zealand has, in scarcely more than a decade, produced wines of equal weight and class. In the rest of the New World, it is a good, and sometimes great, wine.

Scheurebe. Invented in 1913 from a crossing of Silvaner and Riesling, this is an exotic and not particularly long-lived wine, with intense apricot aromas and flavors.

Sémillon. Blended with Sauvignon Blanc for most dry white Bordeaux and used in larger proportions for the dessert Bordeaux, Sauternes, and Cerons. Vinified and aged similarly to Chardonnay in Australia, with similar results, although a more traditional style of the wine in that country offers little oak and fascinating stony flavors.

Seyval Blanc. A French hybrid with crisp, citric character and pleasant drinkability, it's grown well in the middle and eastern United States. England has had even greater success with this grape.

Silvaner. A grape of fairly modest means, except in the Franconia region of Germany and in Alsace. In these two areas, it is textured and full, but with softer impressions in the nose, rather than strong varietal aromas.

Trebbiano. The ubiquitous grape variety of Italy and the basis for Cognac and most Armagnac. Probably the world's most prolific vine in terms of yield, it is still more often used for making brandies rather than wine.

Verdicchio. A classic Italian variety of the Marche on the eastern coast of Italy, Verdicchio produces bright, lemony wines with high natural acidity.

Vernaccia. Several different grapes (including red) are grown in Italy, which bear this name. Although probably not related to the Italian Vernaccias, the one seen in America is called Vernaccia di San Gimignano, named after a town in the province of Siena in Tuscany. Italian Vernaccia is typically crisp, clean, and slightly orange flavored and can be Tuscany's best white wine.

Vidal Blanc. Orange and peach flavors dominate this Ugni Blanc—based hybrid. In the United States, it shows up in both the popular dry version and the wildly popular sweet version known as "late harvest" Vidal.

Viognier. A rare but cultish grape originating in Condrieu in the northern Rhone Valley. It is now being rapidly planted in California, where it yields good examples showing pungent Gewürztraminer like notes and rich Chardonnay like flavors. The finest Condrieu has not been matched in the New World.

RED VARIETALS

Alicante Bouschet. One of the few grapes in the world with red juice. (The color of most red wines actually comes from the grape skins.) Alicante is used only for blending.

Barbera. An everyday wine made from grapes of the same name in Italy's Piedmont region. Offers juicy fruit notes with low tannins and high acidity.

Blaufränkisch. One of Austria's leading varieties, Blaufränkisch is a good substitute if you're a fan of Pinot Noir, presenting a medium bodied wine with red berry flavors and a touch of spice.

Cabernet Franc. This grape is related to Cabernet Sauvignon, with more fruit basket style fruit and less tannin. Less long-lived than its cousin, Cabernet Franc brings herbal notes ranging from slightly tobacco flavored to pungent leafy. It is used to some extent in Bordeaux, especially in Pomerol, but is even more important in the Médoc as a blender. One hundred percent Cabernet Franc wines are offered elsewhere in the world, notably in the Loire Valley, where Chinon is the pinnacle.

Cabernet Sauvignon. One of the most acclaimed and long-lived of grapes, it is found nearly everywhere in the world but is grown most famously in Bordeaux. In that region, Cabernet Sauvignon is usually blended with Merlot and Cabernet Franc. In Australia, it is often found with Shiraz (Syrah) as the blender. Notes of cherry, cedar, and tobacco predominate, and the grape's abundant tannins sometimes make the wine tough to drink in its youth.

Carménère. Once mistaken for Merlot, today the Carménère grape is most commonly grown in Chile. It produces fruit wines with a distinct green bell pepper note.

Carignan. A blending grape in southern France of little distinction. The exception is at Banyuls, where it yields complex, dry, powerful aged red wines. Becoming increasingly better in quality, this varietal is a major component of many Spanish reds. Carigbab is also found in North Africa.

Catawba. An American hybrid, grown primarily in the eastern United States. Before they became successful at growing Chardonnay and Pinot Noir—the classic varieties used to make French sparkling wine—Americans vinted their "champagne" from the hardy Catawba.

Chancellor. An interesting French hybrid, grown with some success on America's East Coast.

Chambourcin. A hybrid of French origin, known for its soft and fleshy fruit, with good examples coming out of Missouri and New York, as well as Australia.

Cinsault. A fine blending agent in southern France, it is an important component in the world's greatest rosés. South Africa's special variety, Pinotage, is a cross between Pinot Noir and Cinsault.

Concord. A native grape of the eastern U.S., at one time, very popular with home winemakers. Now used more often for making jams and jellies.

Dolcetto. A juicy, grapy, and almost Zinfandel like the variety that achieves moments of greatness in Piedmont, Italy. Best enjoyed within five years.

Freisa. A lovely, thick wine of the Italian Piedmont, with flavors of raspberry and strawberry.

Gamay. Within the confines of Beaujolais, France, the top crus (Brouilly, Fleurie, et al.) can be rich, succulent, and capable of aging ten years or more. Elsewhere Gamay makes a pleasant, fruity wine.

Grenache. This grape has many homes and many faces. In Rioja, Spain, it is the grape second in importance to Tempranillo and can show excellent character just north of Navarro. In southern France and the southern Rhone Valley, it ranges from excellent rosé to pleasance, fruity drinker, while reaching imperial heights in Châteauneuf-du-Pape and, sometimes, Gigondas.

Grignolino. A lightly colored wine of the Italian Piedmont, with terrific drinkability and balance—almost as though red wine had been designed to be drunk like a crisp white.

Malbec. Originally used in Bordeaux as a blending grape, Malbec is now closer associated with Mendoza, Argentina. Produces approachable wines with juicy dark fruit, vanilla, and cocoa notes.

EST. WW 1985
THE WILLIAMSBURG WINERY LTD.
2017
Petit Verdot
VIRGINIA
750 ML

Merlot. Often considered the blending grape of Bordeaux, this variety does impact softness to the wines of the Médoc. But it is the heart and soul of many, if not most, Pomerols and St. Emilions. In the New World, Merlot is widely available in varietally labeled offerings and intensely popular for its fruitiness and soft tannins (when grown with that style of wine in mind). This is a grape that has been nearly as successful throughout the world as the Cabernet Sauvignon.

Montepulciano. A thick and enjoyable wine from the Abruzzo and Marche regions in Italy.

Mourvedre. Generally overlooked but nonetheless great, this grape offers wonderful fruit and earthiness in Provence and the southern Rhone region in France. Spain and the U.S. also produce exciting versions.

Nebbiolo. Perhaps the finest grape of Italy, Nebbiolo, offers rather soft versions, as well as the monster agers of Barolo and Barbaresco. These tough and unyielding versions can improve the thirty years or more when from superior vintages, exhibiting aromas of cherry, tar, and flowers when mature.

Petit Sirah. Not to be confused by Syrah/Shiraz, Petit Sirah has found its home in California, where it produces full-bodied wines with high alcohol content and tannins.

Petit Verdot. A minor Bordeaux grape, but one which first growth producers swear by. It is lean and leggy, with a good long-time requirement for it to mature. Petit Verdot has found a home in Virginia and become a favorite at the Williamsburg Winery.

Petit Noir. The classic red grape of Burgundy, a model that intrigues and tantalizes winemakers around the world. Its rich fruits and earthy aromas combine with low tannins for a wine that is almost always drinkable no matter how young. It is, however, finicky and touchy, and most regions of the world still struggle with the grape in search of high quality. Pinot Noir is also an important component in many styles of sparkling wine and Champagne, adding structure, flavor, and in the case of Blanc de Noir—styles, color.

Sangiovese. The primary grape of Chianti, with several well-known clones: Brunelli, the grape of Brunello Montalcino; Pignolo, the grape of Vino Nobile di Montepulciano; and the cultish Sangioveto, perhaps the finest of Chianti's clones. Its sweet cherry and leather tones, when ages, are pure grace at their best but austere and charmless when the wine is poorly made.

Scuppernong. An amber-colored, native American variety. This grape was named for a river in North Carolina and is the basis for much of the home-style wine produced in that region.

Syrah. The grape of northern Rhone, where some of the world's finest wines (Hermitage, Cornas, Côte Rotie) are pure renditions of the grape. Grown also in other countries, Australia (where it is called Shiraz), has pushed it to similar heights.

Tannat. Tannic, thick, and intriguing, it is the grape that gives good substance to the wines of Madiran, (the neighbor of Bordeaux, & the home of Armagnac) and is a favorite in Uruguay.

Tempranillo. The most important grape and the soul of Rioja, Spain. It has rich, dark flavors and decent age ability. Tiny amounts of Grazuelo used in Rioja bring smoky lushness and age-worthiness to the blend.

Tinta Cão. One of the gems of the thirty-four legally allowed grape varieties of port. Other varieties used in the making of port wine include Tinta Barroca, a soft and friendly wine grape; Tinta Roriz (also called Tempranillo and one of port's finest grapes); and Tinta Amerella, a full-bodied but somewhat bland variety.

Touriga Nacional. One of the primary grapes of a great port, it also appears as very good dry red wine. Touriga Francesa is a separate grape variety, but equally important and respected.

Zinfandel. The grape is used most often to make blush wines. The origins of Zinfandel are subject to much debate. One theory has it originating in eastern Europe (as the Dalmatian variety Plavac Mali) and brought to California by wine pioneers as early as 1834. A genetically identical grape in Italy known as Primitivo was almost certainly imported from America in the late 19th century. Thanks to the popularity of the white, or blush, version, Zinfandel has been California's most widely planted variety. Grapy, and bursting with bright, raspberry fruit, it is food-friendly and ages fairly well.

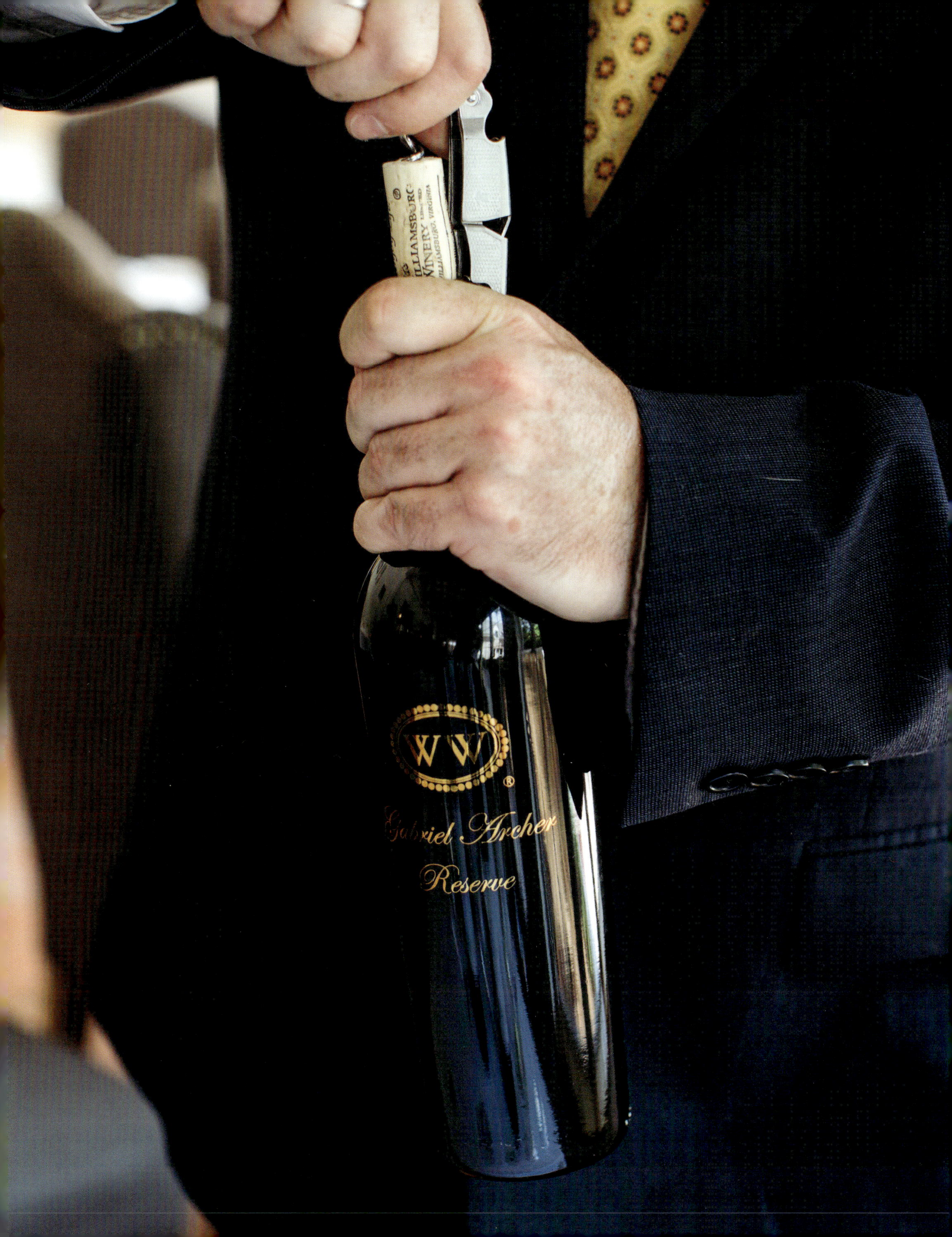
WW
Gabriel Archer
Reserve

Matthew Meyer is sniffing a Reserve wine that has been decanted.

WINES AND AROMA COMPOUNDS

Wine is meant to be enjoyed with the nose as well as the palate.

Enologists (professionals engaged in the study of wine and winemaking) have identified some 700 different aroma compounds in wine. This complexity had led winemakers to develop tools, such as the Chardonnay aroma wheel, to help them better identify the aromatic characteristics of various wines. In the winemaking process, certain aromatic dimensions may be specifically targeted. In the case of Chardonnay, for example, enologists and winemakers typically will strive to control the vegetative aromas, such as grass or hay, and enhance either the crisp, fresh fruit flavors or the mellow flavors associated with butterscotch and honey. Or they may seek a combination of both.

The wine aroma wheel is more complex and is used by analysts in panel evaluations of wines. The wheel shown here lists only a few of the hundreds of wine aroma compounds that have been identified so far.

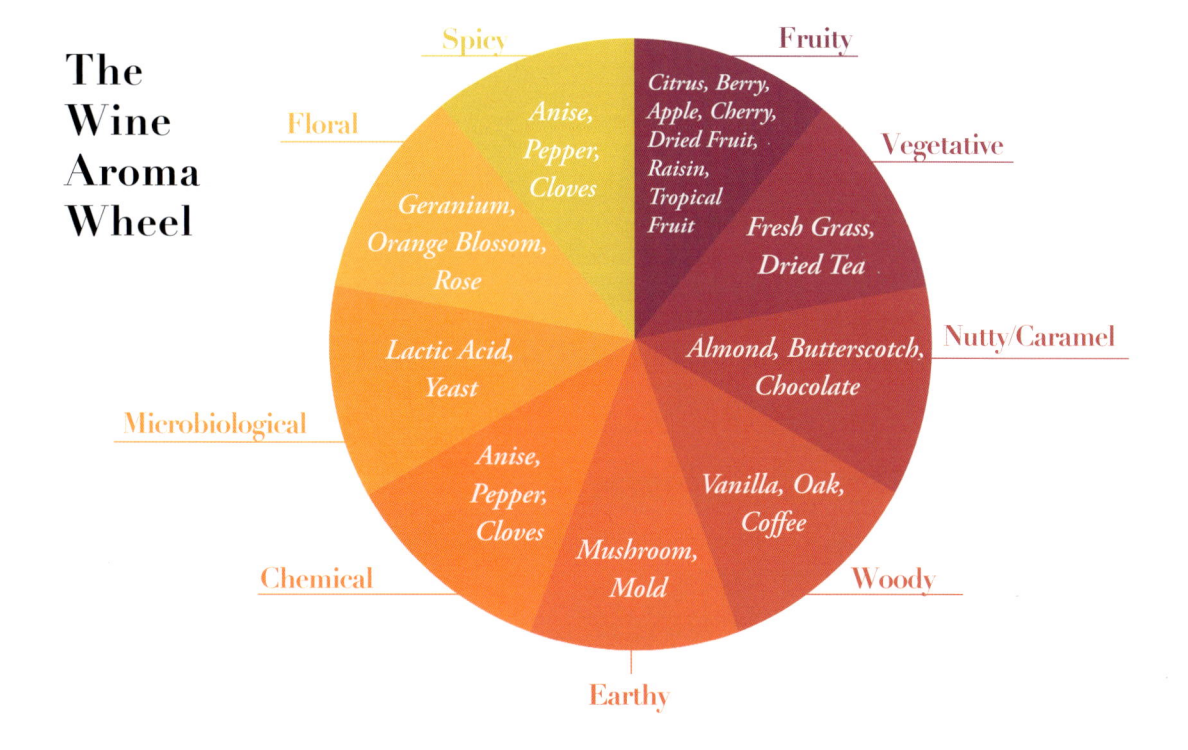

The Wine Aroma Wheel

- **Fruity**: Citrus, Berry, Apple, Cherry, Dried Fruit, Raisin, Tropical Fruit
- **Vegetative**: Fresh Grass, Dried Tea
- **Nutty/Caramel**: Almond, Butterscotch, Chocolate
- **Woody**: Vanilla, Oak, Coffee
- **Earthy**: Mushroom, Mold
- **Chemical**: Anise, Pepper, Cloves
- **Microbiological**: Lactic Acid, Yeast
- **Floral**: Geranium, Orange Blossom, Rose
- **Spicy**: Anise, Pepper, Cloves

The Chardonnay Aroma Wheel

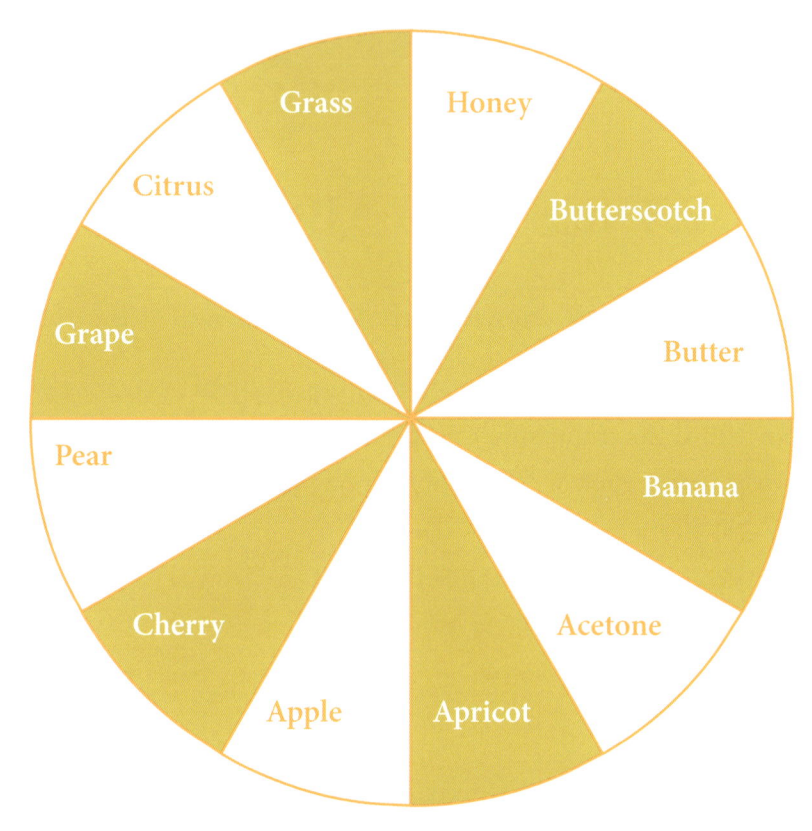

- Grass
- Honey
- Butterscotch
- Butter
- Banana
- Acetone
- Apricot
- Apple
- Cherry
- Pear
- Grape
- Citrus

The Wine Aroma Chart of the Main Grape Varietals

These aromas are not necessarily experienced all at the same time but may become discernible as the wine evolves in the glass.

AROMAS	FRESH FRUIT	FLOWER	VEGETABLE	CONFECTIONARY & DRIED FRUIT	SPICES	GRILLED	ANIMALS	OTHER
WHITE GRAPE VARIETALS								
Chardonnay	Apple or Tropical	Honeysuckle	Linden Tree	Nutty	–	Warm Bread	Butter/Dairy	Mineral
Sauvignon Blanc	Elderberry	Iris	Currant Leaves	–	Sage	–	Musk	Flinstone
Riesling	Grapefruit	Dried Flowers	–	Apricot	Light	Dried Fruit	–	Flint/Petroleum
Gewürztraminer	Leechee Nut	Rose	Geranium	Gingerbread	Nutmeg	Dried Fruit	–	Honey
Marsanne	Pear	Acacia	–	Apricot	Mild	Nuts	–	Licorice
Viognier	Apricot	Violet	Blond Tobacco	Gingerbread	Sweet	–	–	Beeswax
Chenin Blanc	Grapefruit	Acacia	Hay	Pear Butter	Nutmeg	Almonds	–	Honey
RED GRAPE VARIETALS								
Cabernet Sauvignon	Currant	Peony	Green Pepper/Cedar	–	Cloves	Smoke	Leather	Cocoa Beans
Merlot	Breadfruits	Rose	Wood Undergrowth	–	Vanilla	Smoke	Musk	Truffle
Pinot Noir	Cherry	–	Sandalwood	Brandied Cherries	Nutmeg	–	Venison	Truffle
Gamay	Raspberry	Peony	Fruit Pit	Strawberry Jam	Pepper	–	–	Candy
Cabernet Franc	Raspberry	Rose	Green Pepper	Strawberry Compote	Mild	–	Fur	Licorice
Syrah	Currant	Violet	Cedar	Dried Black Cherry	Pepper	Cocoa Beans	Venison	Truffle

Adapted from a French wine document.

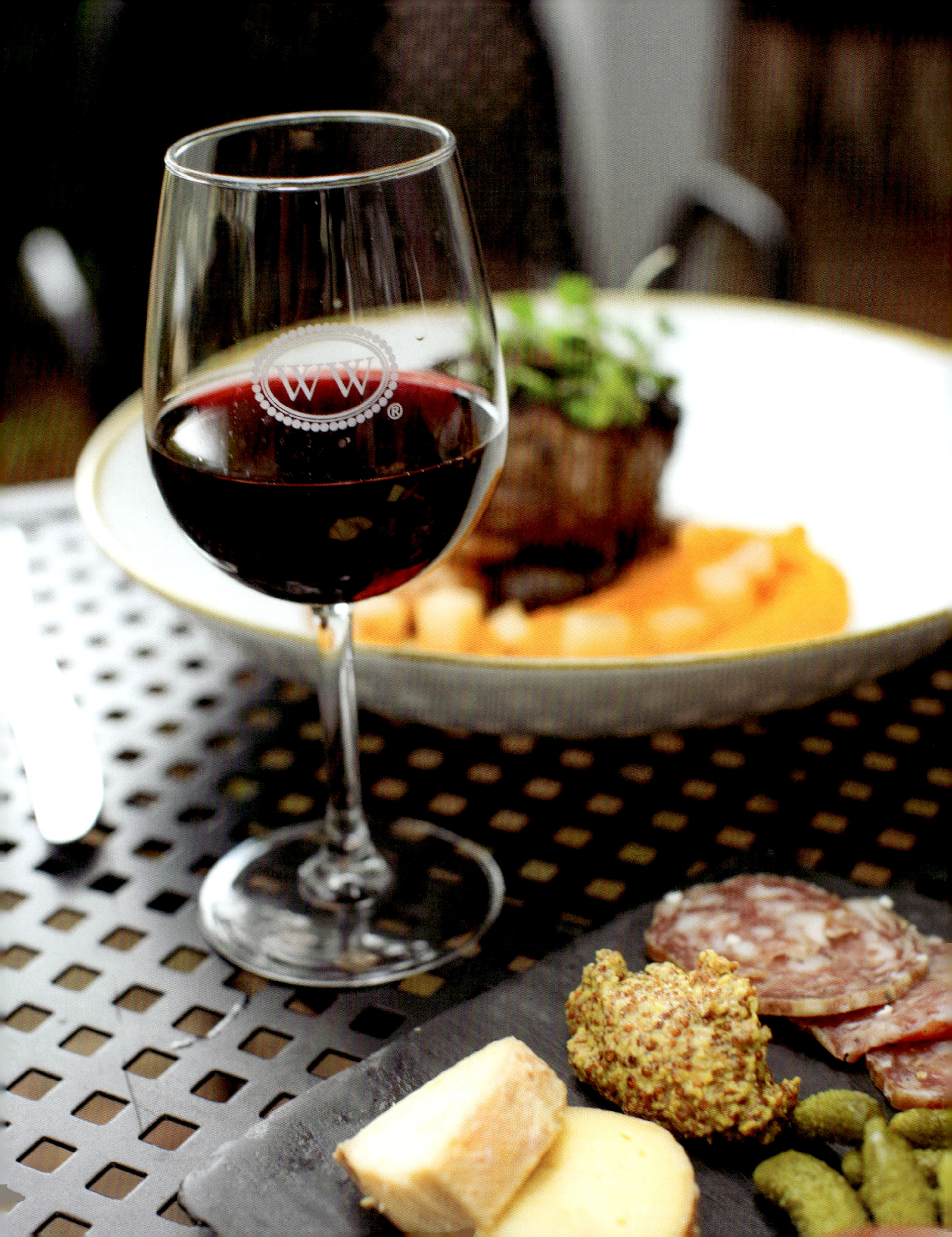
WW

A MARRIAGE OF WINE AND FOOD

The French gastronome, food and wine critic Curnonsky, once remarked that "the marriage of food and wine" was "a more satisfying experiment than the union of man and women!" Although he may have outraged French romantics, he devoted his life to the search for and documentation of exquisite culinary marriages, adapting the principles of such noted culinary masters as Antonin Caréme, J.A. Brillat-Savarin, and Auguste Escoffier.

In that spirit, the chart on these pages is presented as a simple guide to the "Body and Weight" of white and red wines. Alongside the wines, samplings of some of our favorite foods are offered that follow the same pattern from light to rich and heavy.

The specific characteristics of the wines — structure, body, and balance — traditionally have been matched with the characteristics of the foods offered as complements. These matches of textures and tastes were not always based on similarities, but were inspired, at times, by the old adage that "opposites attract."

While so much of the 19th century truths remain true, much has evolved for consumers and in traditions of marrying food and wine since then, the Williamsburg Winery's Matthew Meyer and Patrick Duffeler believe.

Whereas the 15 white wines, 2 Rosé, and 15 red wines that are made at the Williamsburg Winery could be categorized as light, light-medium, medium-light, medium, medium-heavy, and heavy, it would not be beneficial for a person to enjoy wine to be guided by seeminly arbitrary categories.

"Our goal is to make old-world style wines in a new world location that captures what we believe is so critically important in wine, elegance, the identity of the fruit, and the flavors that last in the after taste," Meyer says.

Just turn to the World Atlas of Wine, which includes the Williamsburg Winery, to know just how many options you have to marry food and wine.

Great chefs like Paul Bocuse and Alain Ducasse have been also excellent wine guides in today's world. Many more chefs may be cited and you can count on them to make the right suggestion on marrying the right wine for fine food.

Light Bodied White Wines

Soave and Orvieto: *Pasta Tossed on Olive Oil with Basil*
German Gewüztraminer: *Asparagus with Fresh Herbs*
Semi-Dry Riesling: *Raw Oysters on the Half Shell*
Muscadet: *Cold Poached Fish with Herb Dressing*
Dry Riesling: *Puff Pastry Shell with Wild Mushrooms*
Chenin Blanc: *Spinach and Scallion Quiche*
Champagne: *Fresh Beluga Caviar on Toast Points*
White Bordeaux: *Grilled Scampi with Herbed Butter*
American Sauvignon Blanc: *Grilled Chicken with Tarragon Sauce*
Gewüztraminer: *Duck Breast Salad with Vegetables*
Sancerre and Pouilly-Flume: *Escargots in a Garlic Butter Sauce*
Chablis: *Gruyere Cheese Souffle*
Gavi: *Pasta with Vegetable Cream Sauce*
Macon: *Fresh Trout in Butter and Lemon*
Riesling and Sylvaner: *Alsatian Choucroutte*
Meursault and Puligny-Montrachet: *Chicken Breast in Truffle Sauce*
California Chardonnay: *Fresh Bluefish in White Wine Sauce*
Condrieu: *Tuna Sauteed with Capers and Shrimp*
Barsac and Cadillac: *Poached Pears*

Full Bodied White Wines

Sauternes and Monbazillac: *Foie Gras Frais*

Lighter Bodied Red Wines

Beaujolais: *Grilled Salmon with Fresh Dill*
Valpolicella: *Fresh Pasta alla Romana (Ham and Peas)*
Dolcetto: *Ricotta Ravioli with Tomato Sauce*
Cote de Beaune: *Grilled Veal Chop with Mushrooms*
Rioja: *Grilled Calf's Liver with Onions*
Barbera: *Potatoes, Corn, and Cheddar Chowder*
Chianti: *Foccacia with Tomato and Goat Cheese*
Montepulciano: *Tortellini in a Mushroom and Sour Cream Sauce*
St. Emilion and Pomerol: *Roast Duck*
Cote de Nuits: *Roast Veal Kidneys with Mustard Sauce*
Medoc: *Roasted Venison en Chevreuil*
California Merlot: *Entrecote of Beef with Bearnaise Sauce*
Zinfadel: *Tenderloin of Hare with Wild Berry Sauce*
California Cabernet Sauvignon: *Beef Tenderloin Chasseur*
Rhone Varietals, especially Syrah: *Roast Saddle of Lamb with Garlic Puree*
Brunello: *Hearty Sausage and Vegetable Stew*
Barbaresco: *Roast Squab with Truffles*
Barolo: *Hearty Beef Stew with Winter Vegetables*
Amarone: *Venison Tenderloin*

Full Bodied Red Wines

Port: *Chocolate Truffles*

EST. WW 1985
The Williamsburg Winery Ltd.
2019
Semi-Dry Rosé
VIRGINIA ROSÉ WINE
750 ML

Part 2

– A History of Winemaking in Virginia

– A Brief History of Wessex Hundred

– The Williamsburg Winery at Wessex Hundred

– Wine and Mathematics

– The Wonders and Wisdom of New Technology in Winemaking

© Morphart/Adobe Stock

THE HISTORY OF WINEMAKING IN VIRGINIA

The first Englishmen to establish a permanent settlement in America did so on Jamestown Island in 1607. Almost as soon as they landed, Virginia's earliest settlers turned their attention to planting revenue-producing crops. They were at first encouraged by the abundance of native grapes they found growing all around them. But after years of frustration with the taste of the wines produced from these grapes and the difficulties of growing the European varieties, the average planter—who meanwhile had discovered a real cash crop in tobacco—became thoroughly disenchanted with the notion of winegrowing. However, the challenges that caused the majority to eventually give up would only serve to fascinate and inspire the few who were determined to succeed.

Early support for the idea of winegrowing in Virginia was strong and came from several quarters. In 1619 the House of Burgesses convened in Jamestown to enact the first laws of the colony. The Twelfth Acte made it mandatory for landowners to "yearly plante and maintain ten vines, until they have attained to the arte and experience of dressing a Vineyard, either by their owne industry or by the Instruction of some Vigneron. And that upon what penalty soever the Governor and Councell of Estate shall thinke fit to impose upon the neglecters of this acte."

The Virginia Company, financial backers of the New World venture at Jamestown, were extremely desirous of getting into the highly profitable wine trade and sent vignerons (winegrowers from Europe) to Virginia in an attempt to develop a wine industry here. In 1623, the House of Burgesses increased the required plantings stipulated in the original Twelfth Acte to twenty vines for every male in the family above the age of twenty, demonstrating that the authorities at least were still hopeful about England's prospects of becoming a major wine producer through her colony in Virginia. However, it would be tobacco and not wine that would thrive.

In 1769 An Acte for the Encouragement of the Making of Wine was passed in the colonial capital of Williamsburg. The marker still stands on Penniman Road, where an experimental vineyard was established for the planting of European varietals. It lasted only eight years—until the money ran out, the Revolution began, and the colonial vineyardist was at a loss to deal with phylloxera, climatic unpredictability, and black rot. Still, there were those such as Thomas Jefferson who would keep alive the dream of a viable wine-producing industry in Virginia.

John Adlum (1759-1836), known as "the father of American viticulture," was a veteran of the Revolutionary War, surveyor, and judge, who after a highly successful and financially lucrative decade exploring, surveying, and mapping the frontiers of Pennsylvania and Upstate New York, began to experiment with various grape varieties early in the 1800s. When Major Adlum, as he was known, moved to Maryland, he bought land at the head of the Chesapeake Bay near the city of Havre de Grace, where he celebrated Native American varietals.

John Adlum authored A Memoir on the Cultivation of the Vine and the Best Mode of Making Wine, published 1823, explaining his methods, and urged the planting of vineyards. In 1828, Adlum on Making Wine was published.

Toward the end of his life, he exchanged letters with John Adams, Thomas Jefferson, and James Madison. For over twenty years, John Adlum championed American wine, and his Rock Creek vineyard was an essential stop for wine lovers.

We were able to secure two of the original surveys signed by John Adlum that had been done for a famous Dutch cigar family Schimmelpenninck that wanted to purchase land in Pennsylvania for tobacco planting. These surveys are in our company visitor video room along with other artifacts.

In contact with the Adlumia Society of DC, we received a rendition of the portrait of John Adlum, which was used to create the label for the John Adlum Chardonnay wine.

Interestingly, the Catawba grape varietal favored by Adlum thrived in Ohio in the middle of the nineteenth century, as evidenced in this photo and excerpt from American Heritage provided by Diane Race, who worked with the Williamsburg Winery for fourteen years.

Catawba Grapes, Cincinnati

In 2006, conservator Ralph Wiegandt flipped on his Zeiss stereomicroscope peering at an 1848 daguerreotype, a rare five and a half foot long eight plate panorama photograph of the Cincinnati waterfront.

Extraordinary details from the image jumped out, including groups of men and laborers on the town's outskirts picking bushels of grapes.

Nicholas Longworth had established America's first successful vineyard on that hillside, creating a sweet wine out of Catawba grapes.

According to records, within a decade of this photograph, Cincinnati area vintners were producing more than 600,000 gallons of wine.

Excerpt of the plate showing the vineyard on that hillside. Source: American Heritage, Fall 2011, page 68.

When living in Upstate New York in the seventies, besides purchasing French imports on a regular basis, I occasionally got a bottle of Catawba. I had my father, a real wine connoisseur, sample it. He found it interesting but somewhat too sweet for his palate.

By the 1800s, American hybrids (crosses between European and native American species) had been accepted as the future of grape growing in this country, and most Virginians had entirely given up on the purebred European varietals.

For the next fifty years, up until the Civil War broke out, Virginia would achieve a fair amount of success in the hybrid wine industry. After the war, a comeback was attempted, and Virginia producers even won awards for wines they entered in the Paris Wine Competitions of 1889 and 1900.

In 1920, however, a legislative deathblow was dealt to the Virginia wine industry in the form of Prohibition. Virginia was five years ahead of the rest of the country in banning the manufacture and sale of all forms of alcoholic beverages.

It was not until 1960 that a renewed interest in raising wine grapes began to emerge in Virginia. Mostly American hybrids were planted at first. The 1970s saw success with French hybrids, and in the 1980s, vinifera vineyards began to prove their viability. During that period, the founding of the Williamsburg Winery demonstrated once again in the determination of pioneers by winegrowing and winemaking in the James River region. This time, thanks to the help of accumulated wisdom, science, and modern viticultural practices, they were successful.

While most of Virginia's vineyards are located in the hilly central and northern regions of the state, the vineyards of the Williamsburg Winery are planted in the sandy, clay-rich soils of the James River basin. Having carefully assessed the potential impact of the site's soil and climate on the vines, the fruit, and the juice, the expert team at the Williamsburg Winery adopted a procedure to assure the production of top-quality wines. We feel especially privileged that we can create fine Virginia wines right here in Williamsburg— in the same area where the first serious efforts were made to establish a winegrowing industry in America.

Vineyard with new plantings in the snow.

Today there are some 2,100 acres of vinifera vineyards and nearly 400 acres of hybrid vineyards in Virginia and some 300 active farm wineries.

There are eight distinct Virginia Appellation areas within the various regions:

1. Monticello AVA – Central Virginia
2. Northern Neck George Washington's Birthplace AVA – Chesapeake Bay
3. Eastern Shore AVA
4. NorthernVirginia and Middleburg AVA
5. Shenandoah Valley of VA AVA
6. North Fork of Roanoke AVA – Blue Ridge
7. Rocky Knob AVA – Blue Ridge
8. VA Peninsula AVA – Hampton Roads

VIRGINIA WINE COUNTRY

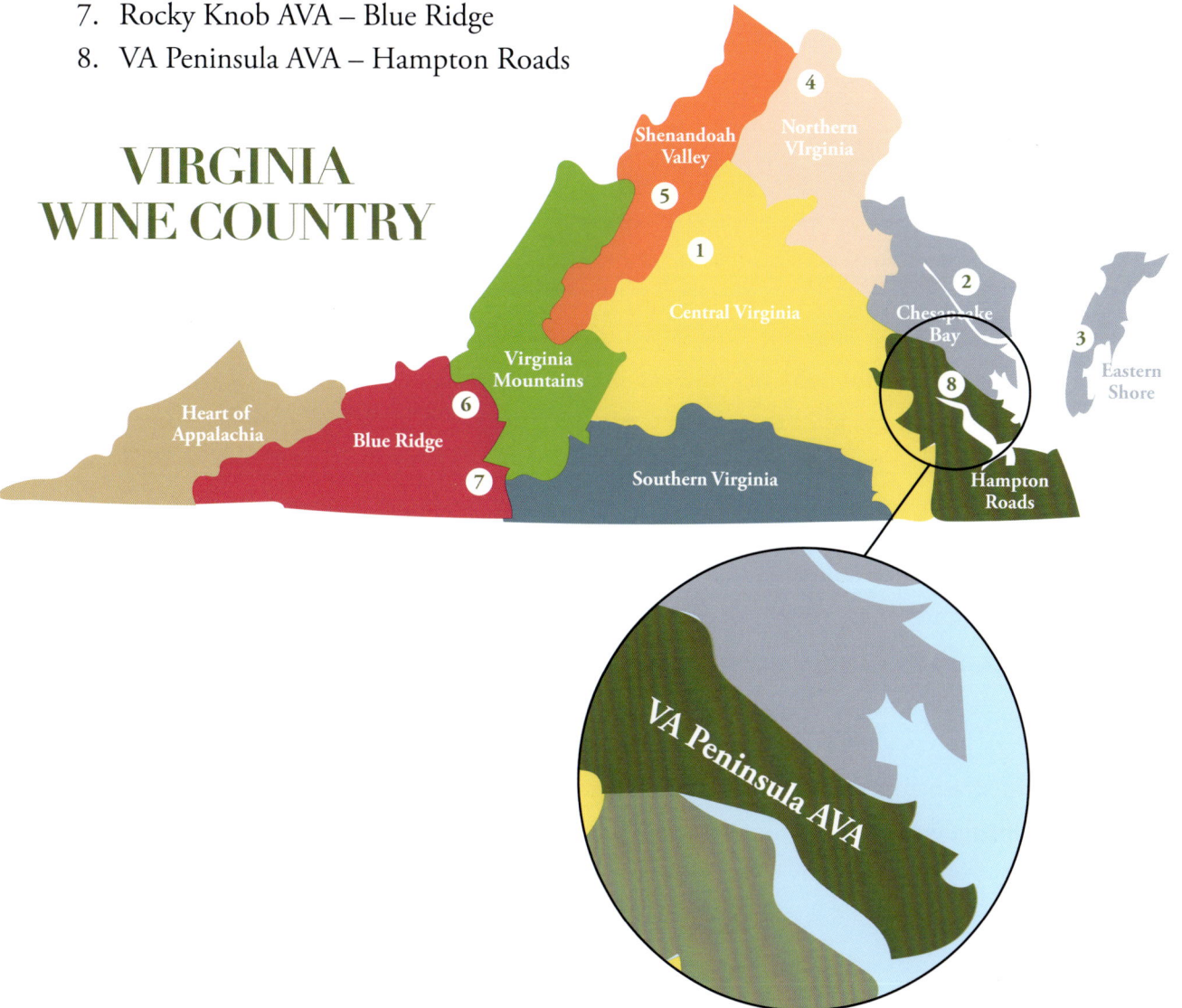

The Virginia Peninsula AVA is the patent that has been confirmed. It was approved in 2020. The application was studied and submitted some five years before.

When studying the evolution of the wine market on a global basis, some important characteristics are worth considering.

In the key wine-producing countries of Europe, Italy, Spain, and France, the trend has been to drink less on a per-person basis but to drink better quality products. One cannot underrate the impact of the visibility and coverage received by Robert Parker; a lawyer turned wine enthusiast who initially extensively reviewed wines from purchases in order to remain independent of the influence of producers.

Export sales of wines from France, Italy, and Spain were significant factors, and by the late eighties, the Parker ratings were fundamental to the marketing success of wineries who wanted to expand their export volume to the U.S.

As the years went by, Mr. Parker went to state wineries and shared his comments with producers that were visited. By the mid-nineties, a number of Bordeaux wineries had in their cellar a special barrel that they identified as the "Parker Barrel."

Mr. Parker has a taste for robust wines exhibiting heavy tannins. It can be said that Mr. Parker also focused his interest on acres that had not been well covered by the international press as in the previous era. He gave the Rhone Valley wines a much more visible image as well-structured wines.

In commenting on the impact of the review as well the writings of wine educators and journalists, one needs to appreciate the importance of the British contingent of writers. The best-known author is, of course, Hugh Johnson, who compiled what was considered the first World Atlas of Wine published in 1971. Equally important is Steven Spurrier, who opened a wine shop right behind the Place de la Concorde in Paris in the seventies and the organizer of the famous "Judgment of Paris" that caused a real shock in the world when top sommeliers could not identify renowned French wines from selected California wines.

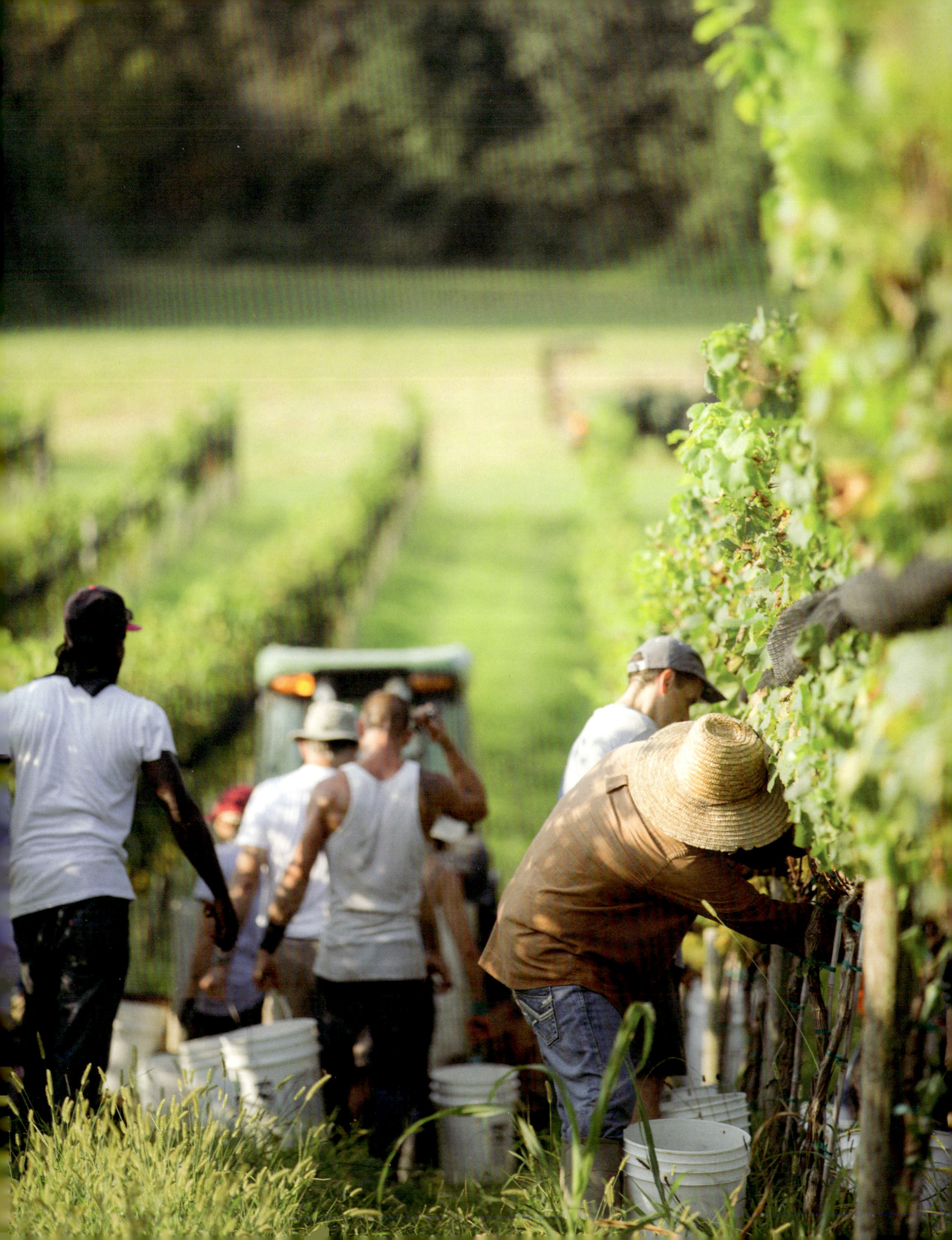

THE WILLIAMSBURG WINERY LTD

2018
Sauvignon Blanc
VIRGINIA

750 ML

A BRIEF HISTORY OF WESSEX HUNDRED

The farm on which the Williamsburg Winery is located is known as Wessex Hundred. The term *"hundred"* dates back to the early days of settlement in the New World. It described a parcel of land that, from an agricultural point of view, could support as many as a hundred families, regardless of the actual acreage.

The first English settlers arrived on the eastern coast of North America in the latter part of the 16th century, landing at Roanoke Island, the famous "lost colony" of North Carolina. None of them survived.

The next major attempt at settlement occurred when three ships left England early in 1607, reaching the Chesapeake Bay several months later. The expedition was sponsored by the Virginia Company, a group of London venture capitalists. It was headed by Captain John Smith and Gabriel Archer, who was co-captain of the *Godspeed*, the largest of the three ships. The other sailing vessels were the *Discovery* and the *Susan Constant*. Gabriel Archer had been trained as a lawyer in England and was seeking his fortune in the New World.

In search of a suitable location for settlement, he led an exploration party up a large river, which was later to be named the James, after the reigning English monarch. He chose a point of land on the northern shore of the stream. His preference, however, was overruled by Captain Smith, who believed that the settlement could be better protected on a nearby island situated two miles upstream from the site Archer had favored. That site became known as Archer's Hope, now the location of Wessex Hundred and the Williamsburg Winery.

As the settlers continued to arrive from England, more small settlements were established along the James River. The area around the original site, then called Jamestown Island, was administered by the Virginia Company under a royal charter granted by King James.

Planter John Johnson settled on a tract of 100 acres of Archer's Hope around the year 1617. In 1621, when the charter of the Virginia Company was revoked, the planters acquired the rights to their land from the Crown, and Johnson paid two shillings for his leasehold. His purchase became the nineteenth land transaction of record in America.

Archer's Hope is a peninsula, a *neck* of land of some 500 acres surrounded by two creeks and two deep ravines. One of its earliest owners was Joachim Andrus (sometimes spelled Andrewes), presumably of German heritage, and the name of the tract became known as Joachim's Neck, eventually corrupted to Jockey's Neck, a name it has retained to the late twentieth century.

At one time, the plantation was owned by Richard Bland, a graduate of William and Mary, who became rector of the Bruton Parish Church. Bland was active in the Williamsburg Community and a frequent participant in the meetings at the Raleigh Tavern, where independence from the British Crown and the creation of a new nation were the hot topics of the day.

Military cartographers onboard French navy vessels transporting soldiers to reinforce Washington and Lafayette's troops during the siege of Yorktown have provided us with some of the best period maps of the Jamestown and Williamsburg areas. One of these maps shows the Bland plantation and the trail leading to Williamsburg. The contemporary drawing on the following pages clearly shows the path to Williamsburg (Number 12)—the main thoroughfare of Wessex Hundred and the Williamsburg Winery. It is recorded that the armies of Maréchal de St. Simon landed on the shores of the James and marched across the farm to rendezvous with the French columns of General Rochambeau and Lafayette at Williamsburg on their way to Yorktown.

From 1785 until the late 20th century, the land on which the Winery is now located was a grain and cattle operation, with a portion having been allowed to go back to woods. The numerous ravines on the farm turned into marshland and have become home to wildlife. Large oaks, copper beeches, and an unexpected cypress grove are to be found on the property. There's an oak tree on the estate that is estimated to be over three hundred years old.

The then abandoned farm was purchased in 1983. To celebrate our common Saxon heritage, we named it Wessex Hundred, deriving the name Wessex, "land of the West Saxons," from the ancient English kingdom ruled over by Alfred the Great.

After considerable research and with the encouragement of the Virginia Department of Agriculture, several acres of Chardonnay were planted at Wessex Hundred in 1985. It was the first vineyard planted in the Williamsburg area since colonial times.

The farm has evolved considerably since its acquisition in '83. The first projects included the elimination of the various automobiles that had been pushed down in the ravines along with the need to relocate the access road to the house dated 1736, which received a serious rehabilitation over the early months of our new settlement. A couple of container loads of furnishings arrived, one from Spain and the other from France, where our two houses had been placed on the market. In '84, the ground for our new house was broken!

There were silos that needed to be taken down, and in '87, the first building of the Winery's operation to be constructed was scheduled.

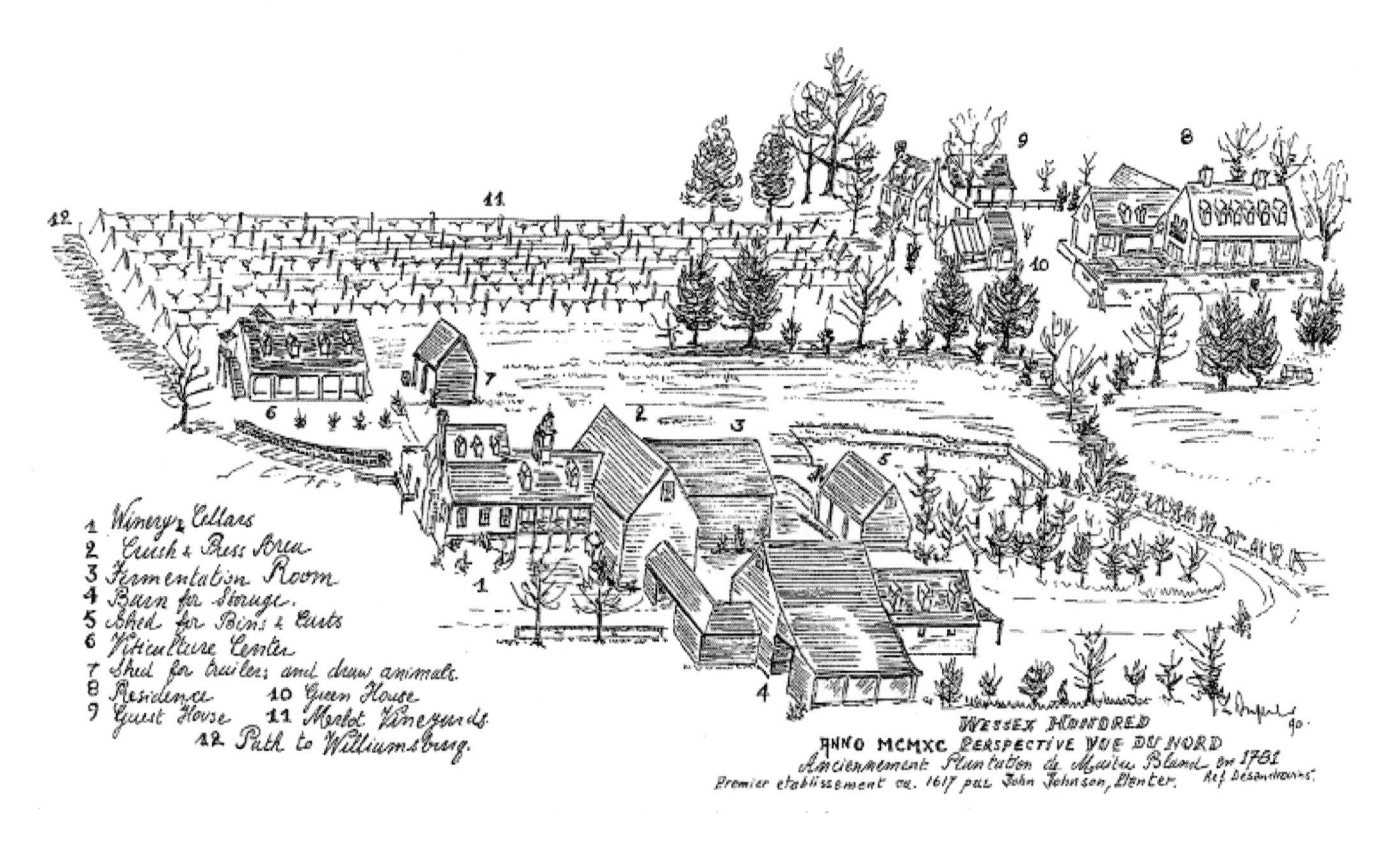

A rendition of the Winery facilities as it looked in 1990.

Immediately afterward, the first harvest was organized in a leased facility in Charlottesville, given that the federal and state winery licenses' had not yet been issued. They were to arrive on November 24th of that year.

During the following year, the farm was to become home of the Williamsburg Winery, a vibrant operation.

By 1989, the decision had been made to dedicate a large portion of the acreage to woods. By late spring, thirty-seven acres had been planted in loblollies with the kind assistance and, importantly, the counsel of Bill Apperson, a professional forester. In '91, another fifteen acres were planted and many more patches to cover. By 2019, another 42 acres of mature copper beech woods could be added to expand the surface of the farm.

Ultimately over these thirty years, over 62,000 trees were planted, and the Pate's Creek southern end overlooking College Creek has been dubbed "Our own Black Forest."

In 2004 and 2005, about 250 acres were dedicated to conservation. The 42 acres, added in 2019, are also deeded to perpetual conservation.

A rendition of the first design of the Winery in 1984 when the thought was to adapt existing barns. It was quickly dropped after looking at the Deloitte Touche financial recommendations between 1985 and 1987.

To the right, the massive oak to the left of the entrance road to the Winery. It was evaluated by Bill Apperson, our Forester friend, to be over 300 years of age.

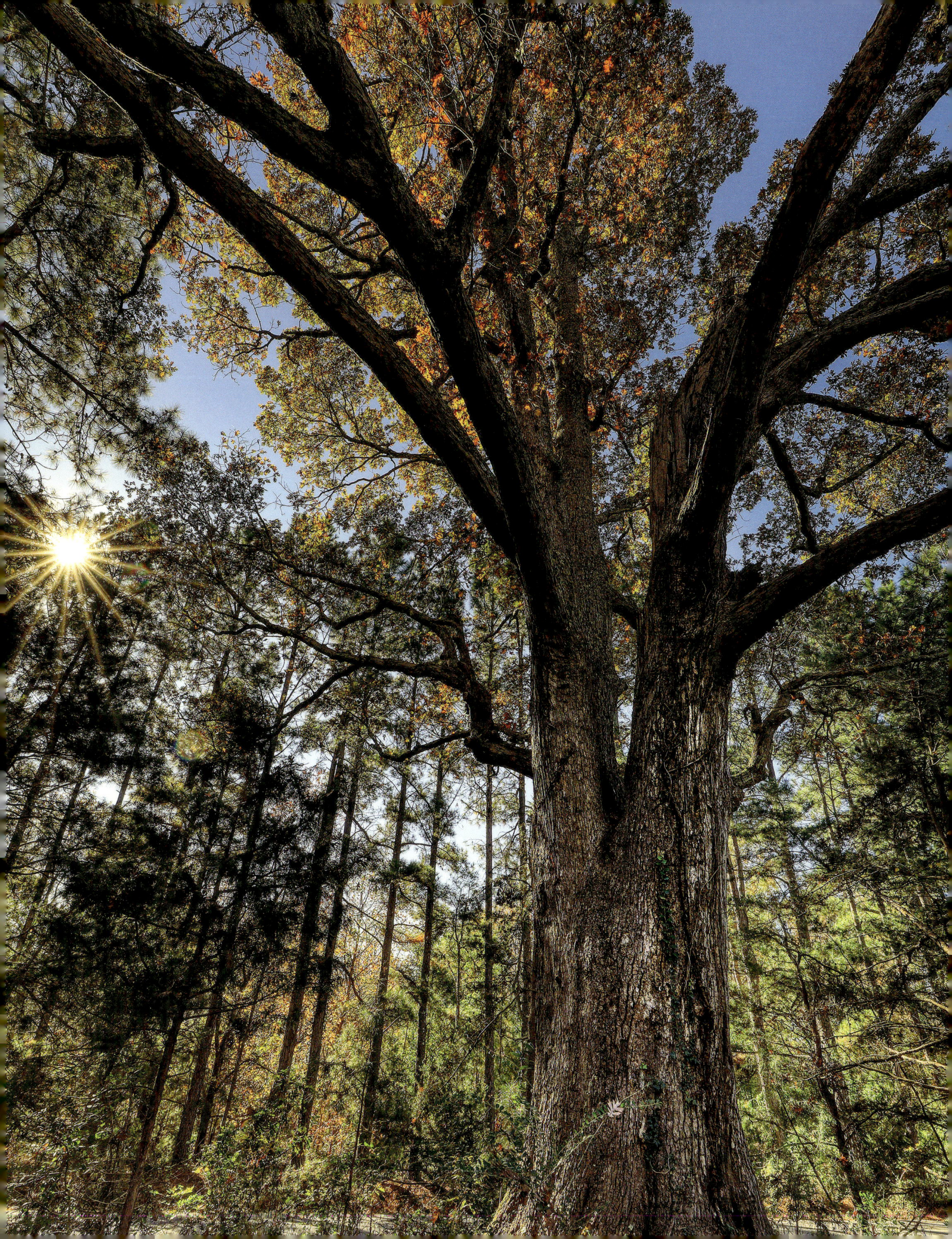

The entrance road to the Winery.

THE WILLIAMSBURG WINERY AT WESSEX HUNDRED

As founder of the Williamsburg Winery, I had been involved in the wine industry in Beaune, the capital of Burgundy during the late seventies. Beaune is a fortified medieval city, still surrounded by high stone walls and portions of its moat. It is the home of the annual wine auction at the Hospice de Beaune, which attracts wine professionals from all over the world. The event takes place in November when the vineyards have taken on their denuded winter look, and a freezing fog can send travelers rushing inside to seek a warm spot in front of the fireplace.

Beaune, in many ways, thinks of itself as the wine capital of the world (and interestingly, so does the Bordeaux area of France). The Grands Crus of the Côte de Nuits, north of Beaune, or the Côte de Beaune, south of the city, have had a long reputation. Charlemagne, the 9th-century German emperor of the Holy Roman Empire, was especially fond of Burgundies and is said to have planted a vineyard in Corton, a small village in the region. The total vineyard surface in Burgundy is relatively small, planted primarily in Pinot Noir, the dominant red varietal of Burgundy. Chardonnay is the varietal of the highly sought-after white wines from Burgundian appellations of Meursault, Puligny-Montrachet, and a few others.

The biggest challenge in developing a winery on the land of the early Virginia settlers was to create an identity that was neither Burgundian nor an East Coast version of a California operation. Wines must reflect their own *terroir*, their unique environment. So must every dimension of the Winery—its style of architecture, its manner of winemaking, its brand of hospitality.

As a point of reference, a Chardonnay from Meursault is all about delicacy, softness, and supple nuances, with a well-structured acid finish under a buttery palate, which will often give it a much longer cellar life than most Chardonnays. George Gallet, the cellar master with whom Patrick Duffeler worked in Beaune, described his Meursault as "grandmother's lace." By contrast, winemakers in California have focused on Chardonnays with rich, massive flavors and relatively high alcohol levels, which can typically reach as much as 15%. The copious amount of California sunshine results in grapes that are heavily laden with aroma compounds.

Virginia wines will never have the fullness of California wines, yet many experts agree that they can be more delicate and complex and that they are more food friendly. There will always be more vintage variation in Virginia than on the West Coast, but that in itself can be an opportunity for the accomplished winemaker to focus on enhancing the personality of each vintage and making sure that the wines faithfully reflect the microclimate conditions under which the grapes are grown.

The major varietals selected for planting at the Williamsburg Winery are Chardonnay, Cabernet Franc, Merlot, Petit Verdot, and Tannat as well as Albariño. Understanding the marketplace and the taste preferences of consumers remain of primary importance in the selection of these grapes.

A rendition in 1989 as the Winery had just been completed and work was continuing in the back as shown on the rendition of the year 2000 on page 87. 1) Retail, 2) Tasting Hall, 3) A small garden over an underground cellar, 4) A warehouse for finished products, 5) Fermentation room, and 6 & 7) The crush area (Note the roof was not as drawn completed).

Richmond Times-Dispatch, Sunday, September 13, 1987 F-9

Williamsburg Winery owners ready for the joy

By Sharon B. Young
Times-Dispatch state staff

JAMES CITY — After nearly three years of anxiety, prayer and hard work, the owners of the Williamsburg Winery are preparing to enjoy the fruits of their labor — literally.

Patrick and Peggy Duffeler, owners of the Williamsburg Winery, said their first harvest of grapes was trucked to a winery near Charlottesville recently to be pressed, aged and bottled.

Duffeler said that nearly 20,000 bottles carrying the Williamsburg Winery label should be available to the public by Christmas, something he said he is eagerly awaiting.

"But we have no illusions," Duffeler said recently. "It will take a very long time to make an extremely high-quality wine because it's a fact that the fruit tastes better as the plant ages, and ours are still comparatively young."

He said it may be as little as five years from now — or as many as 10 years — before he is able to produce a wine high enough in quality to compete with the best of California wines, and possibly those of Europe. In the meantime, Duffeler said, he will concentrate on making the best young wines.

In addition, work is under way on a 16,000-square-foot winery facility that will include a wine-fermenting area, a cellar, a bottling area, a wine-tasting and reception area, a small museum of wine making and office space. Duffeler said the building should be completed by April.

Eventually, the 300-acre farm they purchased in 1984, which is part of what was originally known as Bland Plantation, will be transformed into a showplace, he said. Duffeler plans to use about 200 acres in pasture land for livestock, the winery facilities and a European-style bed-and-breakfast inn.

About 50 acres will be used to plant grapes and 40 more will be left undeveloped for a conservation and wildlife program.

Duffeler acknowledges that the wine-making business seems best suited to someone with loads of patience.

"I've been asked if this isn't a gamble," he said. "I don't know any business that's not a risk, but I've done my homework, proceeded at a careful pace and hired the very best people I could, so maybe I've got a head start."

He said any winery needs a good viticulturist. "That's why we got Jeanette Smith," Duffeler said.

Miss Smith, who has a bachelor's degree in horticulture from Virginia Polytechnic Institute and State University in Blacksburg, joined the Williamsburg Winery last year.

"It was at Tech that I got interested in grape growing from one of my professors," said Miss Smith. "After graduation, I moved to the Finger Lakes region of New York to work in a vineyard there."

After two years in New York, including a stint as a fruit specialist with the cooperative extension service on Long Island, Miss Smith said she wanted to return to Virginia. She met the Duffelers through mutual friends in the wine business.

"It has been great getting in on the ground floor of this and now I'm looking forward to the harvest coming to a close," she said. Miss Smith said she believes the Peninsula can offer a warmer climate for wineries than other parts of the state. Most of Virginia's 11-year-old wine industry is concentrated in the western part of the state.

She said wineries in Virginia can expect less damage to the vines from winter temperatures. The growing season is also slightly longer here, which Miss Smith said gives winegrowers more ease with some of the red varieties used to make cabernet sauvignon and merlot wines.

The warmer temperatures are not without their drawbacks, however. Miss Smith said the characteristically high humidity can make the plants more susceptible to fungal diseases and rot and the hot weather can cause the vines to grow poorly.

For this reason, Duffeler said the Williamsburg Winery uses the drip irrigation method to spur growth. Water from an aquifer is pumped through plastic tubing suspended by wires to 15 acres of grape vines.

A small spigot drips about one-half gallon of water per hour on each plant, conserving water, limiting soil erosion and runoff and ensuring that the water goes directly to the root of the vines.

T-D photo by Sharon Young
Patrick Duffeler, checking his grapes, knows process takes a long time

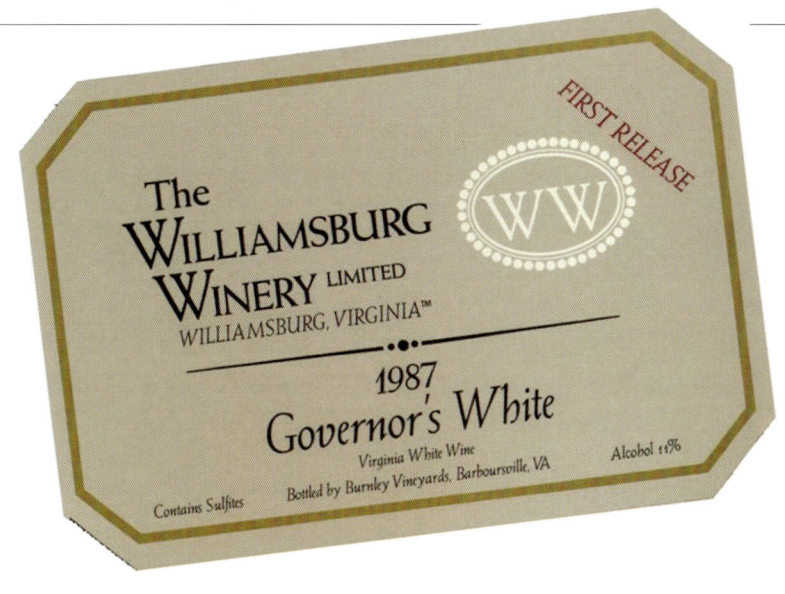

Top: A major article of the Richmond Times-Dispatch of 1987

Left: The label design of the first release of the Governor's White. The wine became a real success.

Right: Governor Baliles presents Patrick with the Governor's Cup in 1989.

To kick off October as Virginia Wine Month, Governor Gerald Baliles presented the 1989 Governor's Cup, honoring Virginia's most outstanding wine, to the Williamsburg Winery 1988 Chardonnay. Patrick Duffeler, owner of the winery, received the award at a banquet September 23.

The very first concepts of a winery structure, as visualized in 1984, were centered around the adaptation of several abandoned barns that were located in the middle of the farm. It soon became evident the barns were no longer structurally adequate and that they would not provide the right facility for producing a product that, after all, needed to meet all the standards of food-grade sanitation. After extensive research and intensive business planning over the next two years, an entirely new structure was designed in 1987. In the meantime, the winemaking operations were conducted in a building that had been erected on the foundation of an old shed. The new Winery was to exhibit a number of traditional colonial features: mixed brick and cedar siding, cedar shake roofs, and a real cupola, accessible from the offices and providing panoramic views of the farm.

The first crush at the Williamsburg Winery took place in the fall of 1987, and the first wines were released in February 1988. *Governor's White,* the first of the Winery's blended wines, was well received in the Williamsburg community, and Tom Powers, the owner of the Williamsburg Wine and Cheese Shop, suggested that it be entered in the Norfolk Yacht Club wine competition. It received the "Best of Class" award at the event, and sales were brisk. *Governor's White* was followed by *James River White,* a more classic dry wine, and *Plantation Blush.* In keeping with their strong interest in history, particularly that of the colonial era, the Duffelers decided that their wines should have names connected with the history and traditions of Virginia. Behind every label on the Winery's list is a bit of research on the part of its owners into the rich and fascinating history of 17th and 18th century Virginia, Colonial Williamsburg, in particular.

That first crush in 1987 yielded only 25,000 bottles, and everything was accommodated in that small temporary Winery, soon to become the viticultural operations center and many years later the Gabriel Archer Tavern.

Footings for the new facility were dug in the spring of 1988. The walls went up in the latter part of June. In late July, the bulk of the equipment rolled in from Scharfenberger of Germany, a family-owned operation specializing in equipment for the wine industry. As French oak barrels were being treated and installed in the cellar, the computerized bladder press, the stemmer-crusher, the pumps, the stainless-steel holding tanks, and the special de juicing tanks were being put into place, while the rafters over the third floor were being erected.

When the last rafter was up, a brief pause in construction allowed in order to observe a popular European tradition: a small tree was nailed to the peak of the rafters to celebrate the completion of that phase of the building and the prospect of years of good fortune under the new roof. Bottles of *Governor's White* were shared by all, but only for a few minutes. The work could not wait.

High-voltage power for the heavy-duty equipment had to be brought in from the main road to the middle of the farm, a distance of over a mile. The utility company had offered a schedule that would connect the new Winery in October. Harvest was anticipated in the latter part of August. After much begging and pleading with executives of the power company, the poles for the power lines were erected in the first half of August, just as the finishing touches were being put on the roof.

Now things were really getting down to the wire. On a Tuesday afternoon, with harvest scheduled for that Friday, the underground cables connecting the power company's transformer to the Winery's electrical box were laid, and the trench was covered. The first test on Wednesday revealed that all of the 220-volt circuits were OK, but the wires for the three-phase heavy-duty current had been overlooked! The winery crew re-dug the trench late that night, and on Thursday, the missing cables were put in place. Local inspection of the connections was approved on Friday morning. On Friday afternoon,

Rendition of the winery facilities by the year 2000. Wessex Hall had been completed in the foreground, and the Viticulture building had become the Gabriel Archer Tavern.

in front of the cameras of a major Virginia television station, the bins of grapes began arriving. The Winery's first major crush had truly been a photo finish.

Readers are encouraged to read the texts of the twenty "blogs" that can be found on the website of the Williamsburg Winery under the "Visit" tab then History & Management. A couple of videos of the TV coverage of 1988 are included.

The crush of 1988 yielded some 8,000 cases, close to 100,000 bottles. The original three wines, now complemented by a Chardonnay, a Merlot, and a Cabernet Sauvignon, were finding their places on the tables of Virginians and of those brave early visitors to the new Winery. The access road was still a dirt trail full of potholes, and one of the members of the Board suggested that the Winery consider augmenting its revenues by securing a car repair franchise!

At this point, there were no good photographs of the Winery and no literature, and without them, attendance at the first festivals became another challenge in itself. Other than letting them sample the wines, how do you describe your winery operation to wine lovers when you have nothing else you can show? The products spoke for themselves; it was true. Nevertheless, the evening before one major event, Patrick Duffeler decided to quickly do a large pen and ink rendering of the Winery on white cardboard. It served its objective well the next day and has been featured on multiple Winery labels ever since.

The Williamsburg Winery team in 1992. Around the table from left to right: Rob Bickford, Dan Uzelac, Theo Holznienkemper, Patrick Duffeler, Tarki Crook, and Peggy Duffeler.

In 1990, as production volume grew, more warehouse space was added in the form of several large barns. More barrels were needed, and more holding tanks. And, most importantly, more quality grapes. That summer, the Williamsburg Winery entered into an agreement with the Virginia Winery Cooperative to manage its winery operation in Culpeper and purchase the grapes from its member growers. The acquisition of Dominion Wine Cellars filled in perfectly with the long-term business plans of the Winery. It provided Williamsburg grapes from various Virginia microclimates.

From the onset, the decision had been made to grow our own fruit here on the winery property, lease additional vineyard acreage around the state, and buy the rest of our grapes on the open market from other Virginia growers. No single location will produce a perfect harvest year after year. The vagaries of weather dictate that each vintage will be different and that they may be true in Virginia more so than in many other places. Giving the winemaker the option of selecting the best fruit from a range of microclimates has contributed to the success of many wine houses in Burgundy. That approach has also served the Williamsburg Winery very well. Ultimately, the decision was made to combine the winemaking facilities, which were at the Culpeper facility and install them in at the third fermentation room in Williamsburg. By that time, virtually all the cooperative producers had closed their viticulture operations due to their age.

Vintage reserves are made only in the best years and from the best fruit. Occasionally a particular vineyard will yield an extraordinary harvest, and that is the time to bottle a vineyard-designated wine. When that exceptionally good harvest comes from one of the vineyards at the Winery, its wine is labeled as estate bottled. Reserve wines at the Williamsburg Winery have been made from fruit that has come from many different Virginia microclimates, including grapes from Suzanne Wescoat's Glebe Vineyard, on the Eastern Shore, as well as from vineyards located in the foothills of Piedmont.

The late 1980s and early 1990s were exciting times for the Williamsburg Winery, as well as for the rest of Virginia's young but rapidly growing wine industry. Patrick and Peggy Duffeler had been guests, along with Robert Mondavi and his daughter, Marcia at an evening hosted by the Chevaliers des Tastevins at Clos Vougeot in the days Patrick was then involved in the wine business in Burgundy. Later, Patrick accepted an invitation to visit the newly constructed Mondavi winery in Napa Valley, where he had the pleasure of lunching outside by the vineyards and comparing notes with California's foremost winegrower. At the same time, the two of them tasted Burgundies and Cabernets. Mr. Mondavi later asked Patrick to participate in the 1991 Kapalua wine symposium in Hawaii as a representative of one of the world's new winegrowing regions.

In 1989 the Williamsburg Winery won the prestigious Governor's Cup award for its Chardonnay. The trophy was presented by the Honorable Gerald L. Baliles, Governor of Virginia. Just a few months earlier, Governor Baliles had officially opened the Winery at a ceremony reminiscent of a tradition dating back to the 17th and 18th centuries in Europe in which the keys to important buildings were presented to the local nobleman. A large rim lock had been installed on the door of the wine shop, unlocked by a large brass key. During the ceremony, a copy of the key was presented to the governor, who, we understand, still carried it on a brass key chain. Gerry Baliles was a strong advocate for the state's wine industry throughout his four-year term. The former governor remained an influential supporter of winegrowing in Virginia and a friend of the Williamsburg Winery.

During these early years, the Winery was invited by *Wine Spectator* magazine to participate in the Wine Experience in New York, received the Critics' Choice Award on three separate occasions, and presented its *Acte 12 Chardonnay* to a large audience of wine enthusiasts. One of the most satisfying moments for the owners and associates alike was when they learned that Robert Parker, America's most famous wine critic, had listed the Williamsburg Winery in his 1993 *Wine Buyer's Guide* as an "excellent producer."

Wines from the Williamsburg Winery have been served at Mama's Fish House, one of the most famous dining places on Maui. Tavern on the Green in New York has served Williamsburg Chardonnay, and Karen Ann King of New York's Union Square Café recommended that dot-com retailers would do well to offer Williamsburg's wines to customers over the internet.

As the years went by, more buildings were added to the cluster of facilities in the middle of Wessex Hundred. In 1996, the Gabriel Archer Tavern was opened, offering light luncheon fare and a chance for visitors to enjoy a glass of wine while surrounded by 360 degrees of green space. The Tavern was inspired by the relaxing atmosphere of yesteryear when time was less constrained. To this day, there are in Europe taverns that have been

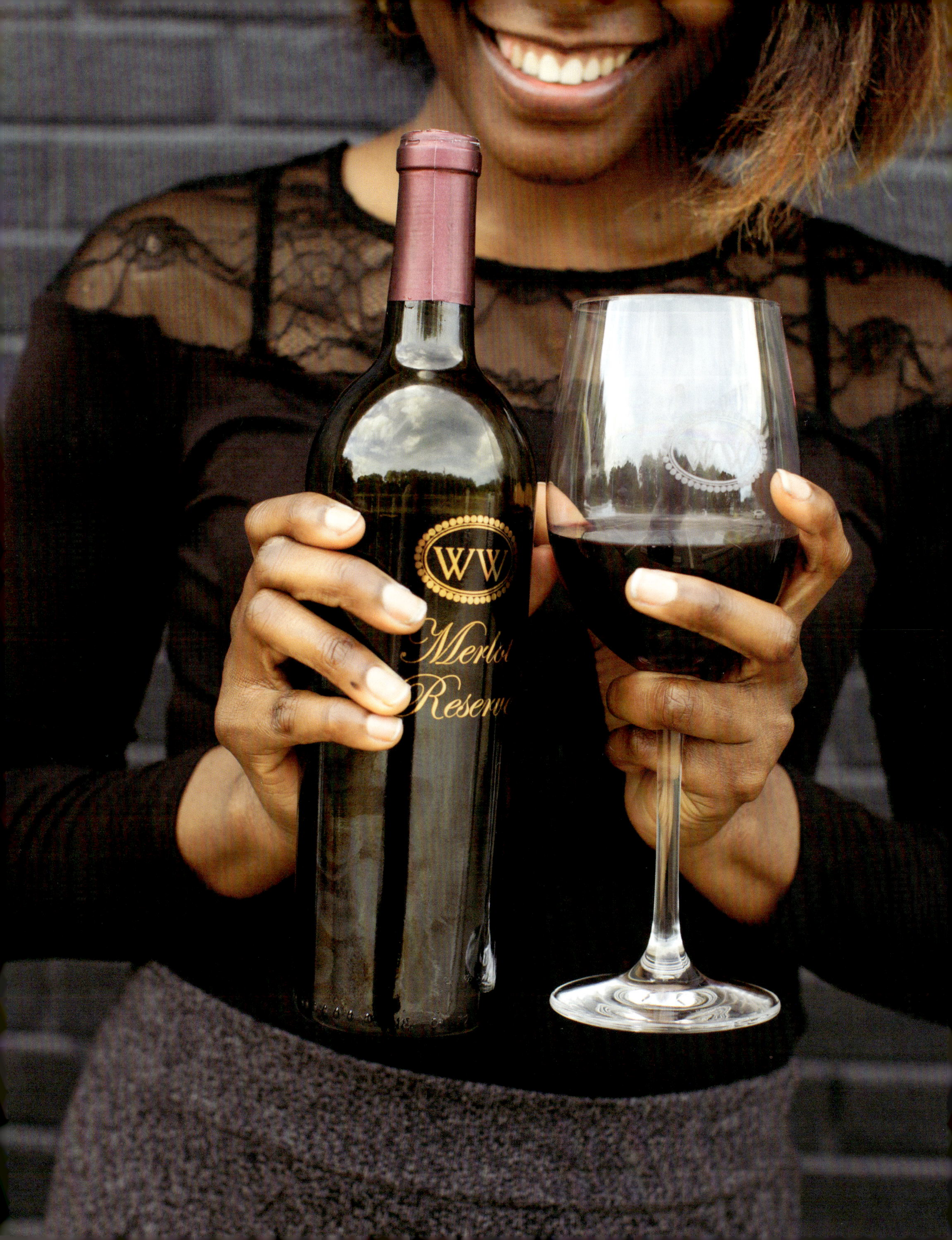
WW

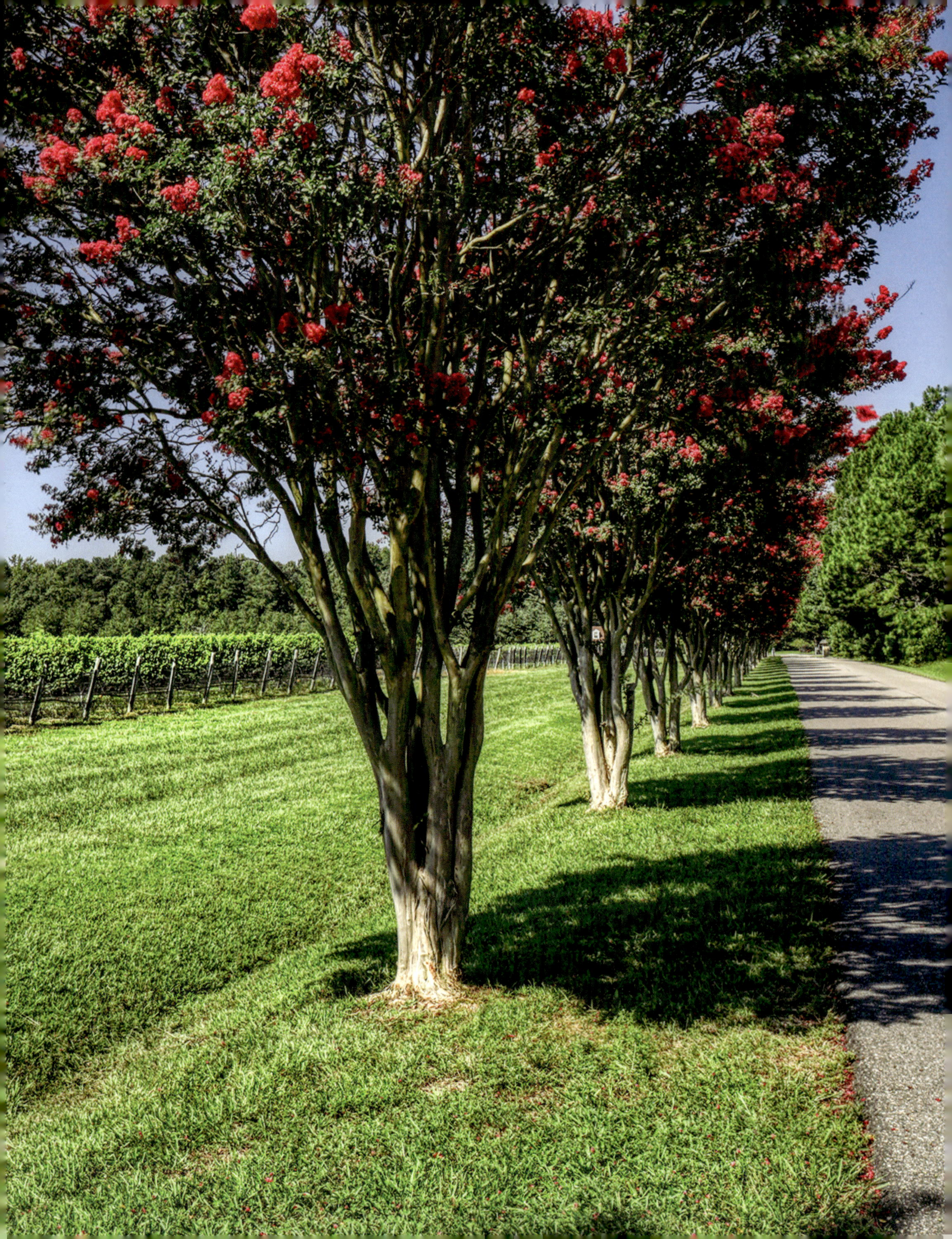

in continuous operation for as many as five and six centuries, where food is grown on the farm and wine is tapped directly from the barrels. At these wonderful old establishments, the modern traveler can enjoy the simple pleasures of healthy fare, excellent local wines, courtesy and hospitality, warmth from the fire in the winter, and cool shade in the summer.

In 1999 the Williamsburg Winery undertook its most ambitious project yet, the construction of Wessex Hall, a three-story building on a footprint of some 9,000 square feet.

Wessex Hall reflects the Williamsburg Winery's practice of blending age-old tradition with contemporary state of the art technology. The architectural design of the facility was inspired by 17th-century cruciform buildings, which featured a large central area flanked by several wings. Details on historic cruciform structures in Virginia, such as Bacon's Castle in Sury, south of the James River, were provided by Bill Kelso, the foremost archaeologist in the state, who now heads the 2007 Jamestown Rediscovery Project.

The roof of Wessex Hall is covered with imported French terra cotta tiles guaranteed to last at least a hundred years. The outside walls are masonry, with a stucco façade. Built on three levels, the new structure adjoins the other main buildings of the winery complex. The basement level includes several barrel cellars, the newest of which is large enough to house 600 barrels, roughly half of the barrel inventory of the Winery. The Reserve Cellar, winemaking offices, a research laboratory, and a microbiology room are also in the basement.

The focal point of Wessex Hall is a spacious event room, ninety-six feet long by forty-eight feet broad, on the main floor. It is available for private and corporate gatherings and can accommodate up to 400 people at a time. Architectural details from the 17th century are reflected in the interior design of the hall, where ten-inch thick posts and twelve-inch wide beams of specially selected timbers support 150 crossbeams overhead. The floor to ceiling fireplaces at opposite ends of the hall came from the Bordeaux area of France.

Made of sandstone, the fireplaces were completely dismantled and shipped across the ocean as numbered blocks. They dated from the early 17th century and were salvaged from two châteaux in one of Europe's oldest and most famous winegrowing areas. They now grace the interior of their new home in one of the world's most up and coming wine-producing regions.

The sparse furnishings in the hall were selected with great care.

Suits of armor purchased in Toledo, Spain, once decorated the dining room of the Duffelers' house in the French Jura. They are replicas of originals from the 15th century and have been installed in the adjacent Susan Constant Hall.

A pair of oak armoires from the early 19th century was discovered in the Ardennes, site of the famous Battle of the Bulge in World War II and shipped over to the U.S. They were supplemented by two dressers and a Spanish armoire acquired over the years in Europe.

The upper floor of Wessex Hall houses administrative offices, a large conference room, and a reception area for business visitors.

Wessex Hall was officially opened by Lieutenant-Governor John Hager at a ceremonial party in May 2000.

In 2002, at the initiative of a member of the Board of Directors, the Company was directed to focus on further developing our own line of wines as opposed to offering our clients Virginia wines along with our selected imports. The focus also shifted from B2B to B2C with emphasis to increase visitors satisfaction.

In 2004, a Special Use Permit was requested from the County to build a special structure that we wanted to call Wedmore Place, a small twenty-eight room hotel to be built just a short walk west of the Winery.

After approval, the equity was raised for the construction of the project, and site work began in '05.

Simultaneously with the efforts to work with the County on the planning for the hotel, we had announced the expansion of the Gabriel Archer Tavern by adding the enclosure of the vineyard room overlooking the adjacent Albariño vines. The Tavern expanded its washroom facilities, the kitchen, and all was connected to County water, and so was the disposal of the greywater.

The hotel was opened in the fall of '07 in the presence of Governor Gerald Baliles and his spouse, Robin who stayed overnight in the Venetian Suite.

During 2001, another extensive facility was built next to Wessex Hall and, for a relatively short period, served as a much-needed warehouse. The planning for the expansion of the facilities for special events, weddings, and functions included the completion of the raised lawn on the southside of the Winery coordinated with the improvements to the large pond linking the storm drain management of the hotel and an XVIII century style canal dug out just south of the raised lawn and featuring an island that was to be connected by a twenty-four-foot bridge.

Ultimately, that facility named Westbury Hall was completed in early 2016 and provides a unique cellar level dining room where guests can see a barrel cellar reserved for Adagio barrels, a space for functions on the main floor with a dramatic stairwell leading to the Bride's room, and a meeting room.

The Adagio wine was created as a super-premium wine in '07 and released for the first time in September '08 just before the onset of the Great Recession. It was well received and has grown to be the flagship of the Williamsburg Winery joining the Gabriel Archer Tavern Reserve, the Trianon, and the other fine wines of the Company.

In order to make efficient storage of wine designed solely for retail, a special shed was constructed in early '18 right across from the visitor's entrance to the retail operation.

As the level of interest by consumers and travelers alike has evolved, and the Company focused on expanding the facilities to provide further enhanced customer satisfaction. The 1619 Pavilion was named as a reminder of the first House of Burgesses' meeting and its "Acte 12" requiring settlers to plant and care for vines. It was built next to three sheds adjoining the Gabriel Archer Tavern and opened to the public in the spring of 2019.

The Pavilion is a twenty-six hundred square foot open air space on a double deck with full coverage next to a terrace featuring tables and umbrellas where beverages from cocktails to wine and beer can be enjoyed.

Numerous expansions of the facilities are under study for construction in the coming years.

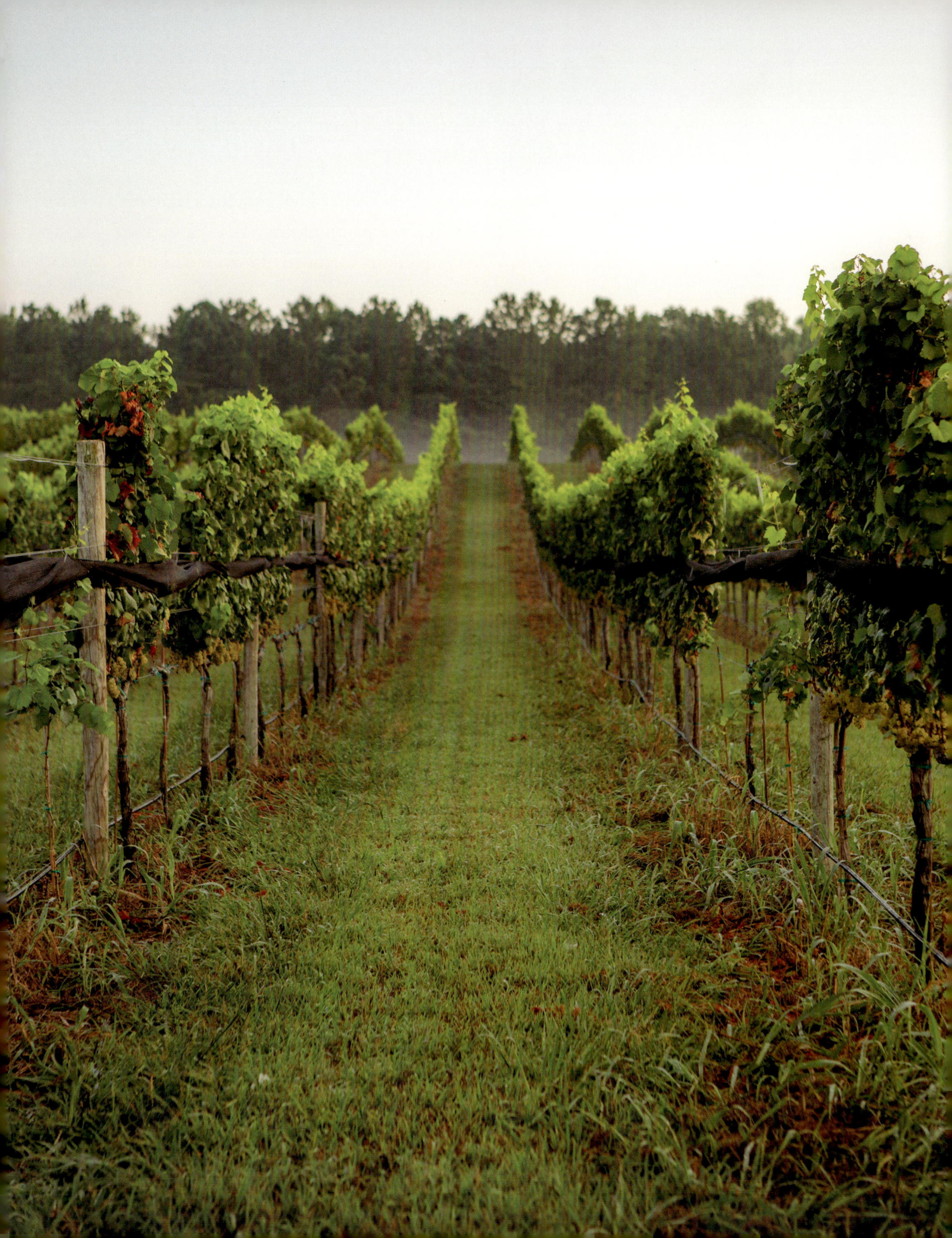

WINE AND MATHEMATICS

One might not think that mathematics, even simple arithmetic, would have much of a role to play in the highly romanticized world of grape growing and winemaking. Yet, numbers are so important to the vineyard owner and the winery owner as they are to any other businessperson seeking to produce a quality product and, at the same time, make a reasonable profit. The winegrower must take many factors into account when deciding how many vines to plant in a given acre of ground, and the number can range from as few as 800 to as many as 4,000. At the Williamsburg Winery, the vines are normally staked four feet apart along the row, with a space of about twelve feet between rows. This generally equates to roughly 600-800 vines per acre.

The targeted yield at the Winery, as well as at other vineyards it owns or leases throughout Virginia, is between three and three and a half tons of grapes per acre of vinifera varietals such as Chardonnay and Cabernet. In the case of certain vigorous hybrids, such as Seyval Blanc, the targeted yield is anywhere from five to six tons per acre. Other numbers become increasingly important as harvest approaches. The Brix level, or sugar content, of the grapes, is closely monitored to ensure that it reaches at least 21° before the fruit is picked. The acidity of the juice is also important, with a pH of between 3.2 and 3.4 considered optimal if the wines are to be nicely balanced.

At the Winery, a ton of grapes will yield, on average, 170 gallons of juice. There is some loss during production and fermentation because of spillage, evaporation (particularly during barrel aging), or other causes. It usually ranges from between 2% and 4%. The standard bottle of wine holds 750 milliliters, and there are twelve bottles to a case. This equates to 2.3775 gallons to the case. With these numbers and a handheld calculator, one can quickly figure the yields on an average acre of vinifera grapes at the Williamsburg Winery as follows:

Per Acre

- **3.0 to 3.5 tons of fruit**
- **552.5 gallons of juice** (average 3.25 tons x 170 gallons per ton)
- **536 gallons of wine** (552.5 gallons x 97% [average loss of 3%])
- **255 cases of wine** (536 gallons ÷ 2.3775 gallons per case)
- **2,700 bottles of wine** (225 cases x 12 bottles per case)

Thus we see that a single vine will yield about 4.5 bottles of wine (2,700 bottles per acre ÷ 600 vines), and a standard 55-gallon oak barrel will hold 277 bottles (55 gallons ÷ 2.3775 gallons per case x 12 bottles per case). To make one barrel of classic, oak-aged red or white wine would, therefore, require approximately sixty-two vines (277 bottles per barrel ÷ 4.5 bottles per vine). Some of the most famous wine-producing houses of Europe and the most successful wineries in America have had such small and humble beginnings. These last few numbers may be of particular interest to aspiring winegrowers who wish to follow in their footsteps.

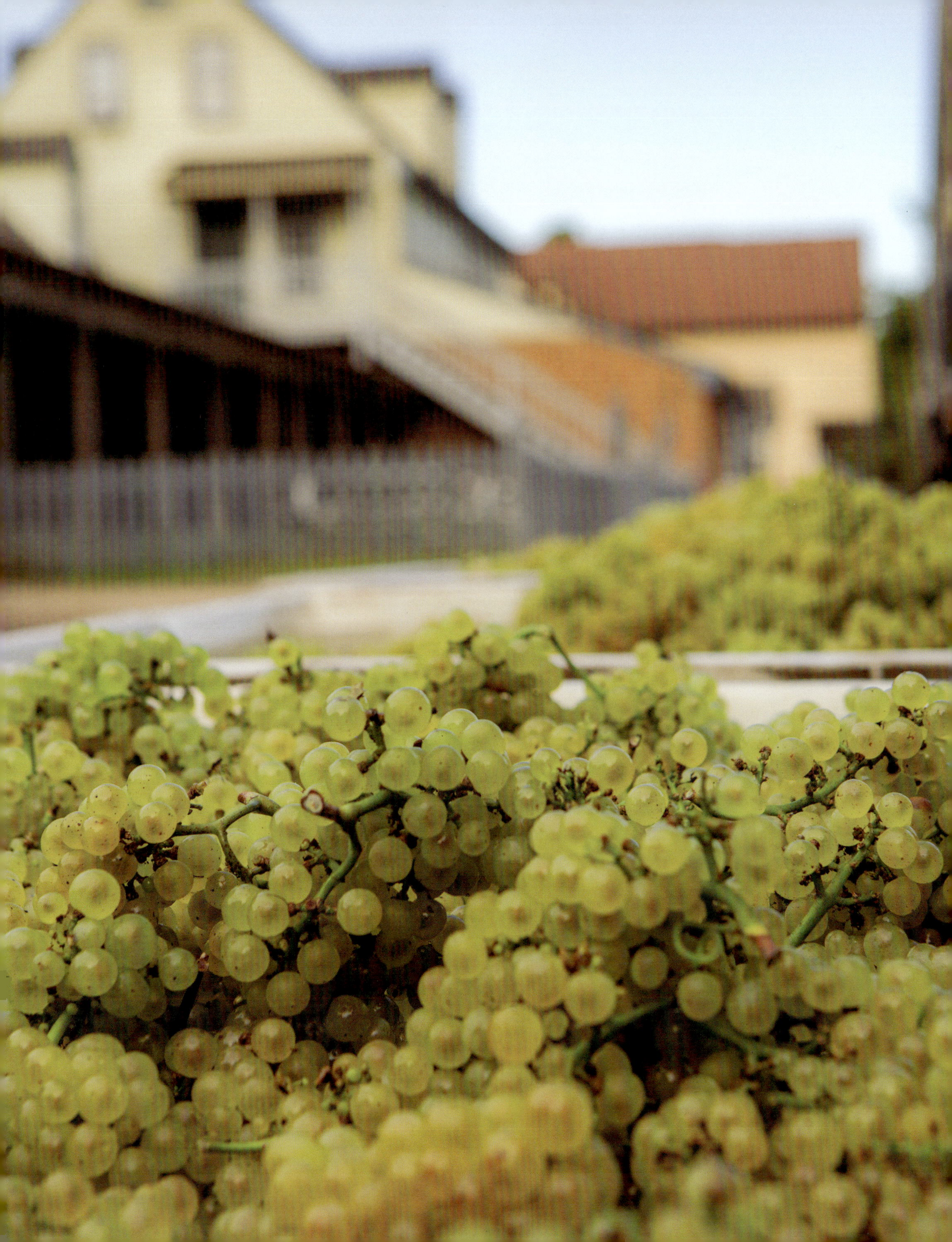

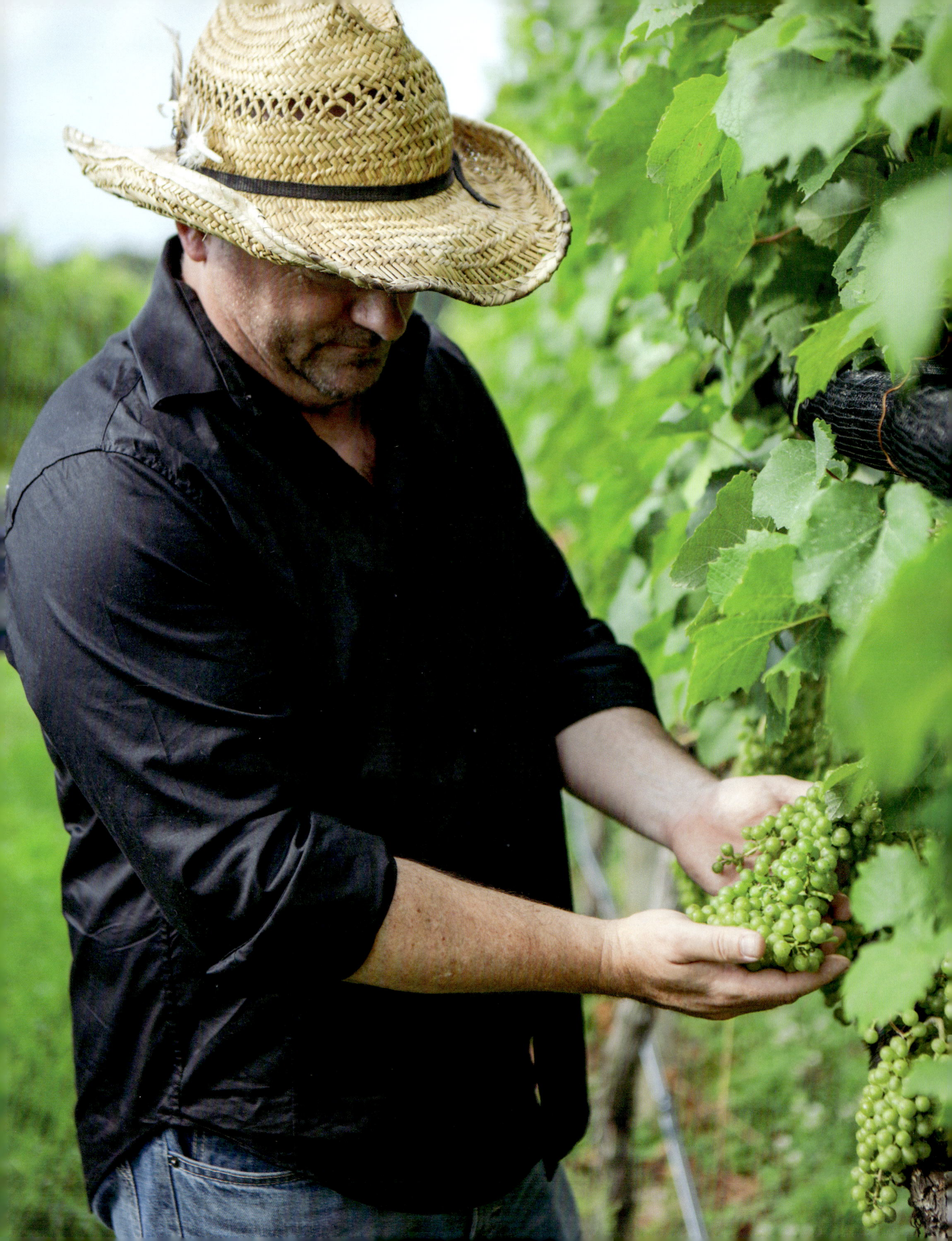

THE WONDERS & WISDOM OF NEW TECHNOLOGY IN WINEMAKING

The first edition of this "Art and Science" was written in 2001. Over the last 20 years, the technology of winemaking has evolved enormously.

Matthew Meyer, the Williamsburg Winery's winemaker joined the team in 2002; consideration was given to replanting many of the vineyards; Matthew selected better clones, and our vineyards were progressively replanted.

Our filtration system then was using a system to pressure the flow of wine through diatomaceous earth. Steve Warner, the winemaker who had performed outstandingly in the 1990s having been a Fresno graduate, also liked the concept of unfiltered wines, but was happy with our then filtration system.

A few years later, Matthew came to me, suggesting that we might need a new filtration system.

When I questioned the wisdom of even a change in our filtration system to Matthew, he said, "Oh, I have organized a trial demo next week." I also asked him what the new filtration system might cost, and his answer was simple – around $70,000.

My quip then was, "The checkbook is closed!"

As the demonstration day came, Matthew was prepared and had a glass of wine filtered with the filter we had, and a glass of wine from the same tank, which had gone through the crossflow filter.

The difference in the taste was evident in the flavors that were expressed.

I turned to Matthew and said, "The checkbook is open."

The crossflow filtration system had been created by a German company during the

AIDS crisis in the 1980s in order to improve hospital blood filtration. That technology became adapted to more applications, including in the wine industry. In Europe, it was sought as a necessity as the disposal of used diatomaceous earth was to be banned by the Commission in Brussels.

The Williamsburg Winery was among the first U.S. wineries to adopt the reverse osmosis filtration system.

That investment in technology continues today with even more investments in filtration systems that have incredible capabilities in reducing volatile acidity in wines, providing more control over the alcohol levels, and in a completely different vein working closely with scientists and engineers (some from NASA) who have provided assistance in gaining a better understanding of the reaction of vines on different soils through aerial photography.

Subsequently, to our contacts with Eric Petiot, a French microbiologist, I learned more about the importance of the organic life of soil and ways to enhance its microbiological life.

After some 28 soil samples from three different on-site vineyards that were dug out at different depths based on the recommendation from Eric, we sent the samples to Mr. Petiot's lab in Switzerland.

His recommendation included the addition of dolomitic powder into the soil by pouring the dolomitic powder in a shank, which has been created between the rows of vines in the vineyards. The dolomitic stone powder is a perfect host for microbiological life.

We will also be studying the addition of ground oyster shells in our vineyards.

A Lees filter has helped us increase the yield of tons to gallons in a small but meaningful percentage.

Over the recent years, there was a discovery in Italy, as we learned, that the shape of an egg is the perfect construction in which, by nature, the liquids will be in constant motion, and that has been of great attraction to winemakers for specialty whites.

We acquired several of these egg-shaped concrete vessels that contain approximately 188 gallons—the constant motion has an effect on the wine.

There are numerous studies under consideration. We may be evaluating the relevance of a new piece of equipment for maceration enhancement.

We also know we need smaller tanks for greater flexibility and limiting the use of larger tanks for small batches.

While traveling in France in 2019, I visited a vineyard where the owner had a robot designed to perform a lot of the labor applied to the vines. We see that technology as a more distant future, but in its time it will improve and facilitate the extensive labor required to maintain a vineyard.

All the applications of modern technology will not and should not be a suppression of the artistic concept in winemaking. The use of technology is meant to be only a help. Too often in modern society, we allow ourselves to be fascinated by technology. We also need to take the time to reflect.

In Clark Smith's *Postmodern Winemaking,* he notes that the science is there in service to art. Old knowledge should be preserved with the objective of putting natural flavors first.

The three concrete eggs.

A toast to our guests seated at a long table between rows in a vineyard.

Part 3

– Behind the Scenes at the Williamsburg Winery

– The People at the Williamsburg Winery

– The Places at the Williamsburg Winery

– Epilogue

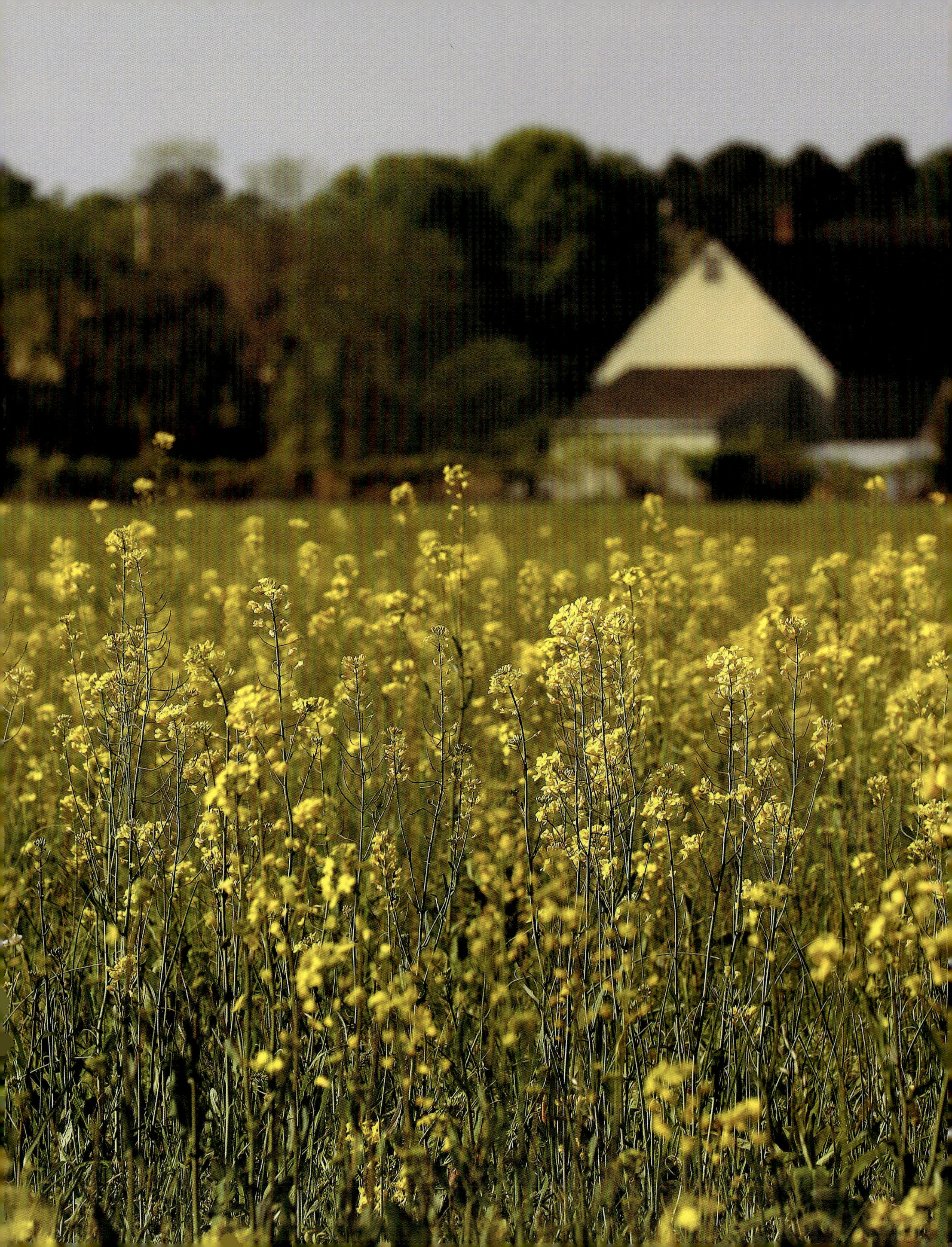

BEHIND THE SCENES AT THE WILLIAMSBURG WINERY

An Introduction

Many years ago, I met a gentleman, Dan O'Brien, who was an outstanding accountant heading a group focused on up-and-coming companies for Coopers and Lybrand, a major accounting firm.

Over lunch, Dan and I were discussing how to approach issues of the Balance Sheet and it became a defining moment for me of how one may look at business.

Dan's comment was that the Balance Sheet does not show anything about the most valuable components in a company, which acutally include the following:

- A list of the customers who regularly purchase the products;
- The list of personnel who manufacture the products and promote them to those customers; and
- The operating system that creates the methodology to hire, organize the manufacturing of products, and control the desired quality standards.

That, for the last 40 years, has been what always occupies my mind when reflecting on the annual audited Financial Statement prepared by our independent accountants.

In the following pages, I hope you'll enjoy getting to know the key officers of the Williamsburg Winery – the PEOPLE – who are responsible for making this PLACE – which is also talked about – so special.

Importantly also is to mention the effectiveness of our board of directors. Since the creation of the company as a Sub S organization, a board of directors was structured to assist and guide management.

During my professional life as an "industrial mercenary," I had been privileged to be

An overview of the farm. To the left various buildings of the Winery complex. To the right, Wedmore Place, the 28-room boutique hotel. The photo is looking south, and in the background is the James River. To the south and east, the forest, which was initially planted in 1989 and 1991 that we call our own Black Forest. The trees are now 35-40 feet tall!

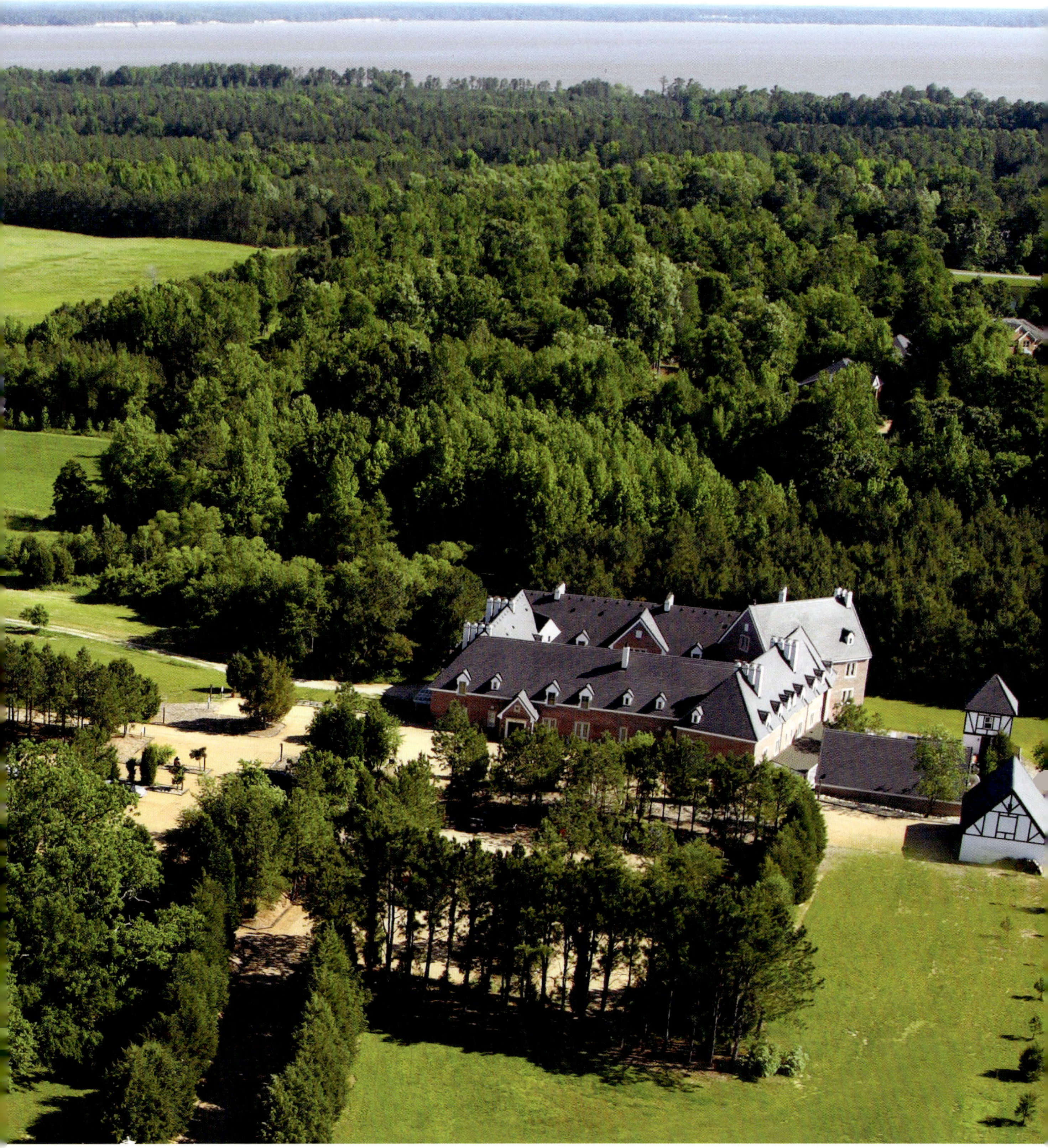

selected to write the text and to select the visuals of the Europe, Middle East, Africa regional president for his presentations at the World Board meetings of Philip Morris and accordingly to be present at those meetings.

Later, when involved in an investment group in Geneva, I was partner and attended all the partners meetings. As the International President of Fragrances Selective, in my CEO capacity, I reported to the board and appreciated the value of boards. The quality of the exchanges during these meetings were always topics to be reflected upon.

The Williamsburg Winery has benefited enormously from a board of professionals with strong experience and also knowledge and appreciation of the complexities of the wine industry. The industry being fundamentally agricultural requires a different mindset. However, whereas the large majority of agricultural products are virtually perceived as commodities. At the opposite end of the spectrum, wine grapes are valued based on quality resulting in very substantial differences in pricing of a ton of berries, say from $500 to $5,000 or even more depending on perceived and measured quality characteristics

The time it takes to grow a vineyard from checking the soil, ordering plants, letting these grow to maturity and generate a good harvest is some five years. From harvest to retail for quality red wines it takes another two years or more. As Marquis Antinori of Tuscan fame once told me during a meeting in NY. "In our industry, you put the cash down and hope to generate cash at least in eight years, or later."

Accordingly, it is a very financially difficult world. But, also, it is a marketing driven world relying on making sure that the products are taste tested by the industry professionals who are quite knowledgeable and issue the ratings which are critical to achieve recognition and demand.

When reflecting on the last thirty years, I think of the contribution of Marc Dash who was a true professional in the world of finance and became my most respected mentor. I think also of Dan Uzelac, previously a VP of Ahneuser-Busch who joined the company in '90, worked as the senior operating executive for five years and is still on our board of advisors today. Marshall Warner, a friend of twenty-five year who arranged to have me join the board of Advisors of his bank when he was in charge of the regional expansion project and now heads the board committee for the future direction of the winery.

On behalf of the company, I am grateful to all those who have given their time and have helped steer this operation.

Looking to the future, I need to place a focus on our long list of relationships. Beginning with visitors and guests, our customers, our many Wine Club members, many who have become friends and call the winery like a home. We are also gratified by having numerous business partners, specialty retailers, fine restaurants that present and serve our wine to their guests.

Other business partners include our vendors and purveyors, our lenders.

In a different light, we enjoy the support of our community that includes so many neighbors.

We have deep relationships with many industry colleagues and very fundamentally we are grateful to our shareholders who believe in what we are building. And, on a more personal note, I am grateful to our living environment, the fresh air we all breathe, the beauty of the vineyards, of the woods of the little creeks on the farm.

For instance, in that long list one name comes to mind, our direct contact to secure fresh oysters for our guests, and also scallops, mussels, crabs. Eating fresh seafood is a part of experiencing quality of life.

The business objectives of our organization are as follows, continue to increase the quality of our wines, enhance our customer satisfaction, increase the distribution of our products, organize major events on our facilities, and in our community and beyond and expanding the range of our offering while maintaining the coherence of our way of doing business, to maintain our healthy orientation such as taking care of our woods, our walking trails

Back to dealing with relationships, over the last eighteen months we have developed a super relationship with Stephanie Heinatz, the founder of Consociate Media, a marketing firm. The group at Consociate is fantastic and they enjoy working with us as we enjoy working with them. Accordingly I asked Stephanie to have her group of professionals write about our team of professionals, about our operation and to capture the real view behind the scene here at the winery in the middle of our Wessex Hundred farm. With my thanks to Stephanie and Rudy Heinatz to line up the photography, the description of the various parts of the business, writing the profiles of the professionals who head the five groups and all the others that are not mentioned who are dedicated and talented professionals and make our business what it is.

The company organization is structured into five groups:

Group I welcomes our visiting guests and organizes the tour and tasting as well as reserve tours and tastings, It also manages our wine club which we are proud to say has about 1,750 members. It also manages the outlet in Merchants Square in the Colonial Capital as well ast the outlet in VA Beach. It operates under the guidance of Kenny Bumbaco, VP of the company

Group II, Food & Wine monitors the Gabriel Archer Tavern and the Café Provençal within the walls of our boutique Hotel, Wedmore Place and overlooks the significant functions business and the many on-site special events. Simon Smith, VP is the leader of that group.

Group III, manages sales to the wholesale-distributors and is responsible for the coordination of the placement of our fine wines in restaurants and many trade sales activities and promotions. Elena Barber, VP works closely with her husband Matthew Meyer, nothing less than the winemaker who has no problem convincing sommeliers and training them in their appreciation of the TWW wines.

Group IV, includes the Financial & Administrative responsibilities, the human relations function, the information technology dimension and works closely with me to oversee the financial planning, the reporting, compliance, relationships with lenders.. From that group, we bring all the VP's together for our regular executive committees, for the product planning committee and also for the general involvement in our marketing committee. Jim Bekert, Exec VP, heads that group.

Group V, covers all Operational dimensions of the company including viticulture, relationships with outside grape growers, all winemaking and the laboratory, bottling, warehouses, distribution, facilities and general maintenance. Matthew Meyer, Exec VP, is in charge of the group.

Rob Ostermaier, one of Consociate Media's talented photographers, is taking shots of vineyard work early in the morning.

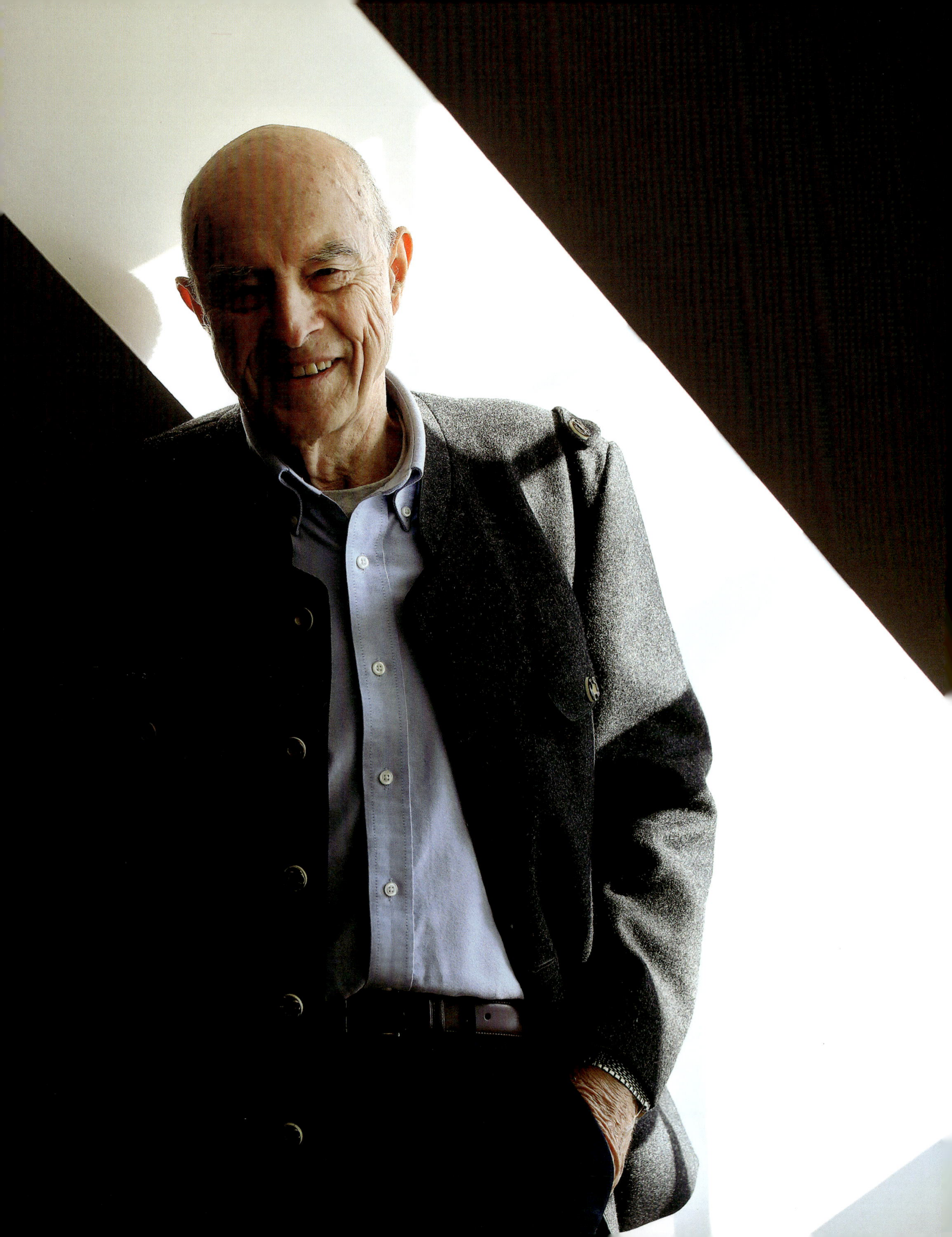

THE PEOPLE AT
THE WILLIAMSBURG WINERY

Patrick Duffeler Cherishes the Moments While Leaving a Legacy

Patrick Duffeler savors what's simple.

Business requires the Founder of the Williamsburg Winery to regularly dress in suit and tie, sit behind a computer and answer a smartphone.

But the Belgium-born executive derives more pleasure from donning military fatigues, work boots and heavy gloves. Disappearing into the 62,000 trees that enrich Wessex Hundred, he can lose himself in the woods for hours at a time, inhaling every breath with vigor and gratitude.

Patrick is as adept at taming a tree with the clippers in his holster as he is making the decisions to grow the Commonwealth of Virginia's largest winery.

Along with numbers, history and literature fascinate him. He is an engaging storyteller who writes with wit. Quick to pick up a pad and draw a concept in need of explanation, he dabbles in art, too. He can cook for a crowd, muse about philosophy, and recite precise dates and details from trips to more than 60 nations. He's been a plumber, roofer, and carpenter at times on Wessex Hundred, able to operate bulldozers and forklifts as easily as he navigates financial software.

Mindful never to boast about his own importance, Patrick doesn't want to be called "Mr. Duffeler."

"Anybody who steps in front of the mirror and thinks he's important is a jackass," he says.

Patrick's professional career began at Eastman Kodak in Rochester, New York, as he graduated from the University of Rochester with a Bachelor of Science in Economics and Finance. Five years after working for the international marketing division, he left to be Director of Promotions for Philip Morris International in Lausanne, Switzerland.

That's where he started the management of a Formula One motor racing team that won two world titles under his leadership, a thrill for a self-described "car guy."

As part of an investment group in Geneva later that decade, he schooled himself in the wine industry in Burgundy, France. He developed contacts in both Europe and California that would prove vital in the upcoming years when he and his wife, Peggy, set out in search of an American farm to be home to them and their sons, Patrick and Terence.

After visiting 52 farms, they settled on what today is the 360-acre Wessex Hundred, home to the Williamsburg Winery, two restaurants and a four-star hotel, Wedmore Place.

Their work to transform the initial property – which he recalls as "a real mess" — never daunted Patrick. His initial treks along the farm's ravines impressed on him the challenges the settlers faced when they arrived in the same spot in 1607.

"I was just nearing 40, Peggy was barely 35, and we had a reservoir of energy," says Patrick, a commuter from his Sixth Avenue office in New York City to Wessex Hundred on weekends until he made Williamsburg his primary residence in 1987.

The Duffelers harvested their inaugural wine in 1987. Two years later, the Chardonnay won the Governor's Cup Award — it remains the Williamsburg Winery's top seller. In 2004, Peggy Duffeler, whose passion for the project rivaled her husband's, died after a long illness. He refers to her as the spiritual mother of the winery project.

In May 2007, Patrick married Françoise Richard, whom he had met 27 years earlier. He affectionately refers to her as his guardian angel.

The Williamsburg Winery accounts for a good portion of the wine production in Virginia

Patrick rises early to start his morning with 400 exercises, 40 pushups included. Fresh air is essential to his daily regimen; he energizes his soul by retreating into the woods to run his hands through the soil and tune in nature's sounds.

Matthew Meyer, a Winemaker with Deep Roots

Family dinner in the Meyer household did not equate to burgers and fries.

At 4-years-old, Matthew Meyer, today Winemaker at the Williamsburg Winery, savored sips of wine at a dinner table where proper dress was expected, understandable perhaps given his lineage. Matthew is the son of Henry Meyer, one of seven Diamond Consultants worldwide along with being a professor at Purdue University.

"Travel, education, culture were important to him, and he instilled that in his children along with an appreciation for food and wine," Matthew says. "Unless you had a note from the Pope or the Queen, you were expected at the dinner table."

It was well known that his mum, Helen Meyer, was an extraordinary cook, making dinner time something to look forward to.

"I spent many hours in the kitchen with my mum stirring pots, pans and licking spoons . . . a memory I shall always cherish."

The British citizen moved to Washington, D.C., as a baby and traveled extensively throughout Asia and Europe as a young adult, fueling an interest in international relations and public policy, his major at the University of Maryland.

Yes, Matthew was a wine geek, too, "But I thought that was just a hobby," he says. Yet at a friend's prodding, he transferred to the University of California-Davis, and completed a Bachelor of Science in Enology and Viticulture, with a minor in Busines and Marketing.

Matthew remained in California for his first four years out of college, starting at Grigch Hills and then later at Heitz Cellars, home to Napa Valley's first vineyard-designed Cabernet Sauvignon, the Martha's Vineyard. He would later take over the Cellar Select Chardonnay program as Cellar Master and Assistant Winemaker.

Matthew moved to the East Coast in 2002 for the position at the Williamsburg Winery he currently holds. Winemaking in Virginia posed a far different set of challenges.

Matthew immersed himself in growing the Williamsburg Winery into an industry leader. His wines earned numerous Double Gold, Gold and "Best of Class" Awards. His signature blend Adagio was awarded the Virginia's Governor's Cup Award, bestowed on state's highest rated wine, in 2014. The Adagio has become one of Virginia's premier wines, receiving multiple 90+ Point ratings from the renowned Robert Parker Wine Advocate and the Beverage Testing Institute.

Humble about the accolades, Matthew offers this wisdom, shared by Joe Heitz, the legendary winemaker behind the Martha's Vineyard Cabernet Sauvignon, considered among the top 10 wines of the millennium.

"Make no mistake about it, young son," Heitz advised "Not one person ever makes a wine. It's a team effort. I didn't make that wine by myself."

Matthew treasures those words. "At a winery like this, it takes a team. I want everybody on my team to be involved and to know what they're doing and why they're doing it. I make sure everybody here is happy and taken care of."

Matthew won't reveal a favorite wine — "All of them are my children," he confides. He and his wife, Elena Barber, also of the Williamsburg Winery, enjoy traveling and socializing with friends, over wine, of course.

Kenny Bumbaco Fluent in the Language of Wine

Kenny Bumbaco studied aboard in Seville for a summer at William & Mary to immerse himself in the Spanish culture.

Languages fascinate him, dating back to his introduction to Latin as a sixth-grader. He's fluent in Spanish, can speak French, some Italian and a hint of Greek.

But at 19, he discovered the language of wine, which opened up an entirely unexpected career path.

"Wine was the most popular beverage in Spain; they're more of a wine country than a spirits country," Kenny says. "I found it fascinating how every single wine tasted so different versus my experiences with beer."

Part of the trip included a sherry tasting.

"At 19, it was my first wine tasting experience," he says.

As a 21-year-old, Kenny sampled varietally labeled wine offerings in lieu of anything that came in a jug or a box. Over the next couple of years, he visited roughly 50 wineries, tasting and educating himself about the winemaking process.

Yet he considered wine a hobby. Graduating with a Bachelor of Arts in Foreign Languages, Literature and Linguistics, the Virginia Beach native continued at the College of William and Mary for his Master of Education.

His desire to teach lasted precisely a quarter at a middle school.

After realizing too many students didn't share his enthusiasm for learning Spanish, Kenny returned to his part-time job from college, assistant manager of The Peanut Shop. He eventually was promoted to manager of the Genuine Smithfield Ham Shoppe in Merchants Square. He created a wine section there, giving him the confidence to apply for a posting from the Williamsburg Winery in the Virginia Gazette.

In 2010, Kenny became the Williamsburg Winery's Retail and Tasting Room Sales Manager. He's held various titles along the way to his current one, Vice President, Direct Wine Sales.

"My teaching spirit comes through when I'm talking to folks about wine. I like doing things like the virtual tasting online and wine seminars in person."

One of his most invaluable experiences came early. In his first year of employment, the Williamsburg Winery founder Patrick Duffeler arranged for him to travel to Napa and Sonoma for training. He increased his knowledge by long hours studying wine literature and joined the Society of Wine Educators. In March 2011, Kenny was named a Certified

EST. WW 1985
The Williamsburg Winery Ltd.
2018
BARREL AGED
Virginia Claret
9% Cabernet Franc, 9% Petit Verdot
WW
Petit Verdot Reserve
EST. WW 1985
The Williamsburg Winery Ltd.
2018
NORTON
Virginia
LIMITED RELEASE
750 ML

Specialist of Wine, a highly regarded certification recognized by the international wine industry.

The Williamsburg Winery also supported his effort to achieve his MBA from William and Mary in 2019.

"My experience in the program really helped me grow from a manager to a leader with the winery," he says. "It helped me learn to think strategically about the goals and objectives of my divisions."

Later that year, Kenny joined the Board of the Virginia Wineries Association, the primary trade organization for wine in the state. He serves on the association's Governor's Cup Committee.

Among the selections at the Williamsburg Winery, Kenny favors the Petit Verdot Reserve. The finish of multiple layers — blackberry, dark cherry, and cranberry along with cocoa and vanilla, and the pleasant earth tones of suede, olives, and a hint of eucalyptus — make it the Williamsburg Winery's most complex wine, he says.

"it's got a nice full body to it, and it really goes with a variety of different foods," he says. "That really is our most standout red out of everything we produce."

Kenny is something of a chef, too, specializing in baked goods and candies — interests that encourage him to hike in and around Williamsburg during his free time.

"Visiting wineries, eating good food and hiking — that's what I love to do," he says. "It's a pretty good life."

Wessex Hundred a Fitting Chapter in the Storied Career of Simon Smith

Simon Smith's career has taken him from one storybook setting to the next.

The Vice President of Food and Beverage at the Williamsburg Winery grew up in lush Kent, England, known for its rolling hills, lush garden and iconic castles. Simon accompanied his father, a designer of homes and hotel interiors, often on travels to Spain, Portugal, Amsterdam and France.

"We dined well and that sparked a passion for me in the hospitality business at a young age," he says. "I actually designed on paper my own hotel. I was about 10, and what I can remember from the elaborate kitchen."

He took his first job, dishwasher in an English pub, seriously. "It was the old school way of being a dishwasher, no machines," he says.

He earned a quick promotion to "salad guy" and then prep cook, enabling him to secure a job as breakfast cook at a nearby hotel. Realizing he needed an education to advance,

Simon completed a hospitality management degree at West Kent University.

Fresh out of college, he was hired by Gravetye Manor, a Michelin Star restaurant and hotel nestled in the forest of West Sussex. In his four years there, he finished a management training program, learning every aspect of the business. His final position, sommelier point steward , allowed him to mingle with an affluent crowd — celebrities including Paul McCartney and Eddie Murphy who would drop 1,000 pounds a night on dinner and lodging.

"That was really icing on the cake," he says. "That took me into the wine world."

By the time he was 21, Simon was the first Brit to be hired in the cellars of renowned winemaker Louis Jadot in Burgundy, France. He lived in a hostel, teaching himself French with cassette tapes while he drove.

"What an incredible experience. I put everything into it you can imagine," he says. "I learned how to be a Burgundian French person."

Napa Valley called him after that. It was 1997 and his words to his mum upon leaving England, "I'll be back in 18 months."

Simon hasn't left the United States since. Other stops prior to the Williamsburg Winery included the Boar's Head Resort in Charlottesville and Blackberry Farm, luxury accommodations in the Smoky Mountains. Three years at Wyndham Hotels & Resorts followed by three years at Bluegreen Vacation Ownership introduced him to the corporate world.

The Williamsburg Winery crystallizes each of those experiences. "It reminds me of Burgundy, it reminds me of Gravetye and of Blackberry — all the places I've been and literally everything I've done," he says. "Here it is nestled in Williamsburg, where there's so much opportunity. It was fitting for me and the Duffeler family was exactly the type of family I wanted to work for. It was a good fit."

Simon oversees Wedmore Place, the Williamsburg Winery hotel, events and the Gabriel Archer Tavern. The avid cyclist also runs the Williamsburg Winery Cycling Club, which member exceeds 500. He logs as many as 4,000 miles annually, time to lose himself in an outdoor, electronics-free world, a mindset he and his wife, Lori, instill in their four children.

"It's so diverse and I love that about this industry," he says. "You can have a plan for the day, and it may get thrown up in the air by the end of the day. It's so much fun. Since I was 14 years old and going back to that dishwasher job, it's the excitement of people, of working with them and trying to make things better every day, that I enjoy. I've got a great team. It's the people who make it. The farm is beautiful, but the people make it."

An Unlikely Return to Her Roots for Elena Barber

Moldova, the birth country to Elena Barber, boasts more wines per capita than anywhere else in the world.

"Pretty much everybody in my country makes their own wine," Elena, Vice President of Trade Sales for the Williamsburg Winery, reveals in her lovely Romanian accent. "My parents made a house wine every year. From the picking to the stomping of the grapes, I was part of all of it as a kid."

Nonetheless, she had no intention of making a future in the industry. After earning an undergraduate degree in public law and an MBA from Grenoble Ecole de Management, Elena worked in the legal department of a human rights organization. Marriage brought her to the United States in 2006, where her focus turned to caring for her son, Chris.

Years later, after a divorce, friends introduced her to Matthew Meyer, head Winemaker at the Williamsburg Winery since 2002. They married in 2011, the same year she commenced employment there.

Elena typically promotes and places wines among a variety of restaurants in the commonwealth, particularly those that embrace the farm-to-table model. During the COVID-19 pandemic, she transitioned to working with grocery stores and other new distributors.

"Every day is different," she stresses.

Elena's unique perspective on wine stems from her roots. Winemaking dates back centuries in Moldova, a former part of the Soviet Union that achieved independence in 1991. By comparison, winemaking is in its infancy in Virginia.

"Virginia is still learning what works well, what grows well, what doesn't do well," she says. "At home they've been making wine for generations."

Admittedly, Elena favors white wines with particular affection for [Albariño](#), distinguished by a burst of lemon to complement the citrus taste, and Petit Manseng, tropical with an aromatic honeysuckle and wildflower layer. Both pair well with oysters and other local seafood favorites.

When not working, Elena finds times to fish and bike and enjoys curling up with a good read. An avid European traveler, she hopes to visit more places within the United States, particularly Washington and Oregon. Along with Romanian, she speaks Russian and a bit of French.

Elena loves listening to people share stories about their own adventures.

"You meet a lot of interesting people when you work in food and wine industry," she says. "That's the main part of why I love what I do."

After 38 Years at One Company, Jim Beckert Makes Himself Home at Another

Jim Beckert knew he wanted to retire in Williamsburg after a visit to Ford's Colony nearly 20 years ago.

He and his wife, Nanette, call it home today, though Jim is far from retired. The Ohio native is Executive Vice President and Chief Financial Officer at the Williamsburg Winery.

It's a position he's held since a real retirement after 38 years at Verizon Communications.

Jim held a variety of roles there, his last, Assistant Treasurer in charge of managing the financial aspects of the company's $42 billion pension and benefits liability for employees, their dependents, and retirees.

"That's 700,000 people," he says.

His affinity for numbers led him to major in finance at the University of Notre Dame, also his father's alma mater. He later earned an MBA at Loyola University of Chicago.

While he stayed with the same company, Jim crisscrossed the nation to work in its multiple offices in California, Massachusetts, Connecticut, Texas, Illinois, Arizona and New York. The last stop was New Jersey, before they moved into a house they had built that overlooks the 18th fairway on Marsh Hawk.

A causal conversation with a member of the Williamsburg Winery Board of Directors led to his initial meeting with Patrick Duffeler, founder of the Williamsburg Winery. "I interviewed and was offered a job the day after that. Three days later, I was here working," he says.

Back when Jim worked at Verizon, a break during the day would send him to Starbuck's. At the Williamsburg Winery, he uses the spare moments to learn from Winemaker Matthew Meyer, Vice President of Direct Wine Sales Kenny Bumbaco and Vice President of Food and Beverage Simon Smith.

Since his March 2019 start date, Jim prioritized understanding every aspect of the wine business, even the tedious details about filter pressures and evaporative loss.

"If I need to explain something to an external auditor, I want to be prepared to do it," he says.

Jim and Nanette will celebrate 40 years of marriage in 2021. They have four adult children and two grandchildren.

In addition to a renewed interest in golf, Jim enjoys the 2017 Merlot, his favorite among the Williamsburg Winery selections.

Meet the Extraordinary Françoise Duffeler

Françoise Duffeler's appreciation for nature and its spiritual ability to nurture dates back to growing up in the picturesque French countryside. Gothic castles, fragrant gardens and acres of bucolic green space distinguish the Loire Valley, luxuries Duffeler never took for granted.

"Even at a young age, I knew how lucky I was," she says.

How fitting that the pastoral vineyards that flourish in the region foreshadow Françoise's future. The wife of founder Patrick Duffeler is a guest on the Williamsburg Winery Board of Directors and a consultant for Wedmore Place, the four-star hotel at Wessex Hundred.

While she didn't envision an American future, Françoise determined at a young age to live a "non-ordinary" life.

Voraciously curious and well-read, she embraced writing and drawing, often sharing her pencil-sketched portraits with others.

"For so many, life has no color," says Françoise, who later studied at the Louvre Art School in Paris. "I wanted to color the life that was given to me."

Françoise attended hotel management school in Bourges followed by internships in hotels throughout France and Switzerland prior to professional positions in Germany and the United Kingdom. A tireless traveler, she has been back and forth to multiple Asian countries, marveling at the limitless array of customs, cultures, and landscapes in each.

One lesson from those excursions resonates among many. Standing amid Ladakh's dry, barren terrain in north India, Françoise could not find a tree.

"I could never live here," she thought.

"I was always conscious of how critical it is to be able to breathe fresh air," she says.

Twice, Françoise climbed the Himalayas in snow, though another trek in the world's highest peaks is the most memorable. She and five others climbed aboard a dilapidated bus, headed to the mountains to meet a refugee Tibetan family that a friend wanted to sponsor. The bus stopped short of the destination, forcing them to cross a forest to reach a Buddhist temple where the family resided.

"We walked and walked in the dark until we finally reached the place," she says. "The following day we were told the forest was full of tigers!"

From the mid '70s until 1981, she worked at several prestigious boutique hotels in the center of Paris near Place de la Concorde, the largest square in the French capital. There, in 1979, she first met a dashing businessman, the head of the creation of the Marlboro Formula One car racing team.

His name was Patrick Duffeler.

They conversed easily — she recalls him driving his car right up to the feet of the Eiffel Tower — and he talked of one day finding a farm in Virginia so his two sons could connect with the homeland of their mother, Peggy.

Françoise and Patrick didn't talk again for 23 years.

She married Danis Bois, who founded the Danis Bois Method, a soft tissue therapy that involves applying gentle pressure while stretching the body's connective tissue. Françoise participated in the creation of a school based on sensorial body care training and later organized seminars and symposiums on behalf of the holistic approach to health. After a divorce, she studied esthetics and remains committed to many of its principles.

On a whim on March 20, 2004, Françoise mailed Patrick a postcard, the front of it an old stone house in the middle of a vineyard. She had no way of knowing Peggy had passed only two days before.

Patrick received the postcard on March 29, and they corresponded regularly. One afternoon, he telephoned her.

"Instantly when I heard his voice, I knew it was him," she says.

After frequent international trips for both, they married in May 2007.

Patrick refers to Françoise as his guardian angel and cherishes her kindness and tolerance. She adores what she refers to as his "original personality."

Together, they are one of a kind.

The Williamsburg Winery Cooking School:

A Celebration of Virginia's Bounty

The object of the Cooking School is to provide an experience, particularly with local producers and farmers or professional advisors such as a nutritionist, a purveyor of quality hams, a grower of oysters, or an organization that imports charcuterie. It's designed to celebrate the bounty of Virginia in collaboration with the chefs cooking talent and organic element of the produce.

A Focus on Reaching Out
FROM 1987 TO THE PRESENT

Returning to the title of this book, I have chronicled the making of wine as both art and science, a multistep process with its roots in the vineyard. The best viticulturist understands the role of nurturing the vines just as a premier winemaker knows when to harvest, which grapes require the most attention, the details of fermentation, when the wine is ready to be filtered and bonded and how long the wine must age for the highest quality product.

These same ideas apply to the relationship building that a winery needs in order to grow, to thrive, to expand its reach. It is no secret that every industry is a people business. Every winery, no matter how good the product, is only successful if building, growing and nurturing relationships remain a priority.

We're grateful at the Williamsburg Winery to have so many strong and valued professional relationships. We have them worldwide. We have them in Virginia. We have them in our own Williamsburg community. They are every bit as important as the grapes we grow and the steps it takes to create a memorable wine. It takes a village to build an identity as we have done at the Williamsburg Winery, and I appreciate every member in it.

We were furiously busy in those early years. We needed to convince a lot of people that we were not making swill and that we were ambitious to reach wine lovers in Virginia and outside of the Commonwealth. Wine auctions immediately appealed to us.

In 1990, Bob Stanton, Founder of the Chesapeake Bay Wine Classic Foundation (CBWCF) Grand Auction, invited us to participate and help in their licensing and in the organization of the event, which is always scheduled around the first days of November. I remember the impact of the first Gabriel Archer Reserve case offered and the bids mounting at one of the first auctions, somewhere around 1993.

We have been active with the CBWCF for all those years and watched with enthusiasm at their highly successful growth. Roughly 200 folks attended their early events. Now they have nearly 1,000 wine lovers enjoying the auction, and the organization has sponsored multiple special events, like the Wine, Women & Fishing Tournament in the summer. The CBWCF generates a lot of money for charities in Virginia and has become the largest wine auction in the Mid-Atlantic area.

We reached out to the Richmond Ballet, which had its auction organized at the Commonwealth Club and at the Jefferson Hotel in Richmond. Thanks to the help of Wilson Flohr, we also worked and promoted Maymont in Richmond.

In the '90s we acquired a vineyard very close to Charlottesville. We were connecting with the management of the home of James Madison, Montpelier, where we sponsored their annual horse race for a number of years.

We also developed a relationship with Poplar Forest and made a private label wine for that organization. There we had a fun evening with "President Jefferson," impersonated by Bill Barker, myself and the audience. The highlight — rather pleasant interview with President Jefferson asking a 20th century winery operator how to succeed.

In 1993, the most influential critic in the wine world, Robert M. Parker, published his 3rd edition of the Wine Buyers Guide, which included a reference to The Williamsburg Winery and a comment on the Acte 12 Chardonnay, describing it as "a particularly impressive wine" (pg. 1056).

In 1997, the famous Morrell Wine Store in New York City issued its fall wine sale catalog, and on page 38, The Williamsburg Winery VRC 95 was noted as a "Must-Buy."

A collection of program and catalog covers from the Chesapeake Bay Wine Classic events over the years.

The Williamsburg Winery was also mentioned in a number of books, such as the American Automobile Association tour book on the Mid-Atlantic; The Insider's Guide to Williamsburg; The Wine of Virginia, a complete guide; The World Atlas of Wine by Hugh Johnson; Beyond Jefferson's Vines; Virginia Wine Country; Wineries of the Eastern States; and Wineries of Virginia and Maryland and others.

In 1998, the Richmond Museum of Art planned to exhibit the Fabergé egg collection with the assistance of Forbes magazine. We sponsored the event and also created a private label endorsed by then-Governor Gilmore.

Throughout the '90s, the wine festivals in Virginia contributed a great deal to the visibility of the industry and received a lot of press coverage. Virginia had the largest attendance at wine festivals of all the states in the country.

Our close friend Gordon Muchie, an ex-foreign service retired, dedicated his life to promoting Virginia wines, traveling to California or overseas with samples of various Virginia wines for people to enjoy.

Michael Glassman, Bob Stanton, Elyse Luray, Fritz Hatton (auctioneer), and Eleonor Stanton.

Board Member Alaura Guion and Executive Director Jennie Capps.

Crowd Shot at one of the auctions and bidders responding to the auctioneer.

Our own Gabriel Archer Tavern opened in 1996 and featured fine wine and food to provide the casual enjoyment of both.

With a 92 rating, we received an accolade from Washingtonian Magazine with the headline Virginia Upsets California.

Inc. Magazine featured a story on The Williamsburg Winery for its success in attracting growth capital that became the stimulant for IBM to invite me to be a keynote speaker at the national promotion under the title of The CEO Experience—bringing us the speakers to CEO's gatherings in Ohio, Texas, San Francisco, and Atlanta. These were the infant days of the development of the internet. It was fascinating to listen to the tech specialists talking about stretching the limits of technology to build the worldwide system.

During the latter portion of the first decade of the new millennium, we brought special car shows to the winery, which was irresistible for me. For three years, we organized Ferrari on the Vines with the Ferrari ownership association. We organized Corvettes for the Vets shows, structured by several of our retail specialists to feature up to 100 Corvettes.

Through all these years, the Williamsburg Winery has supported the military through the USO.

Our organization has been in touch with NATO Allied Command in Norfolk, Virginia. We had a sponsorship with Langley Air Force Base and were selected by the captain of the U.S. Navy George Washington flat-top to have a special edition of our Chardonnay to be stocked in the aircraft carrier for tastings with special visitors when overseas.

We have enjoyed receiving awards and recognition for our wines. The celebrated publications and organizations that rate wines have established ratings based on a 100-point scale with wines in the 70s rated as acceptable, 80s good to very good, and those scoring in the 90s are coded exceptional. In recent years, we have accumulated 34 ratings from 89 to 92. Eight of those were for various vintages of Adagio.

Moving forward, we will be launching the Tour de Virginia for cyclists and have a weekend scheduled for a showing of Mercedes. We have also hosted gatherings of Porsches.

All of these milestones stem from the growing, making and nurturing of our grapes, our wines and our relationships.

Relationships remain critically important for our approach to business. We make wine in a healthy environment. We celebrate our customers and our friends.

Cheers to all!

The fireplace at the west end of Wessex Hall.

THE PLACES AT
THE WILLIAMSBURG WINERY

Classic Fireplaces Add to Wessex Hall's Warmth

Appreciating the essence of Wessex Hall starts with an understanding of open-hearth fireplaces. The Williamsburg Winery's largest event venue houses two at opposite ends of the 48 x 96-feet space.

The Williamsburg Winery's Founder Patrick Duffeler discovered both fireplaces in from destroyed 18th-century houses in the Bordeaux area and had a mason salvage them. Prior to shipping them to this country, he assured each of the fragile white stones was marked in chalk with a number.

"From floor to ceiling, all those pieces had to be put back together," he says. "I had great fun working with the mason on the reinstallation of the fireplaces." Also, translating metric measurements in feet and inches.

The fireboxes for each were integrated with units that originated in Denmark; they are well deeper than what most are accustomed to, and feature large outer hearth extensions in stone.

"You don't have to worry about a piece of spark coming out," says Duffeler, smartly dressed in a Janker while tending to the coals on a bended knee.

A robust fire burns, and Duffeler delights in its whimsy, bemused by the cackle of varying volume and spirals of cinders. The spellbinding effect of the blaze in the open-hearth fireplace speaks to all the senses. It's fragrant but not overwhelmingly so. Minus any screen or tempered glass, the fire emits a heat that warms the skin and invites lingering.

It's hard not to stare at the burning wood in front. With friends, it's an ideal focal point for sharing stories. Alone, it can turn an extrovert into a reflective thinker.

Consider Wessex Hall yet another gathering place to enjoy wine at the Williamsburg Winery.

Wessex Hall hosts as many as 80 events in a year. It's a favorite venue for a wedding reception and can accommodate 180 for a sit-down dinner or as many as 300 overall.

Wessex was an Anglo-Saxon Kingdom in southwest England from the sixth century until a united English state emerged in the 11th century (1066).

Constructed in 1999, Wessex Hall opened the following year. The rectangular space was built in a style classic to Virginia and inspired by the British. The east-to-west length flanked by the north-to-south wings strengthens the resistance of the building to the fierce winds indigenous to the area.

"Those wings symbolize a lot of the construction they would have had in the 17th century," Duffeler says.

Duffeler crafted the front door; he's designed multiple doors during his lifetime. He wanted to replicate a 17th century door and worked with a carpenter to execute it, finishing it off with old fashioned imported nails from Mexico.

What's wonderful about Wessex is its understated elegance. The floor is in aged pine. Duffeler knocks at the 10x10 beams — "solid pine," he confirms. The ceilings are of two different heights. The center one is 12 feet high — in addition to the lovely effect, that's a necessity for the fireplaces at both ends. The ceilings dip to 10 feet on both wings.

More treasures from Duffeler's travels are on display throughout as are replicas of tapestries, including an eye-catching one from the 17th century that celebrates a wine harvest. An early 19th century French mahogany armoire contrasts with a less ornate one that equally splendid. Across the room, more furniture adds to the décor, including a dresser from one of Duffeler's trips to Spain marked by authentic hardware.

Weaponry from the period is on the wall, including helmets and swords.

Wessex Hall spills into what used to be a terrace distinguished by the stucco ceiling. Standing tables and what Duffeler deems "good pieces of wood over barrels" make for gathering spots for wine, hors d'oeuvres and conversation.

With so much wood of varying shades in Wessex Hall, it's surprisingly bright. Windows bring in natural light. Four candelabra chandeliers are breathtaking during the day and even more so at night. Flameless candles illuminate as do smaller unobtrusive lights overhead.

Duffeler aimed for charming and warm light — both achieved and aided by the spectacle each of the fireplaces creates.

"With the two fireplaces going, it throws an interesting light," Duffeler says. "People will naturally want to congregate in front of the fireplaces."

Talk of Wessex Hall always returns to the fireplaces. One German and one French motto is above each in gold calligraphy. Their English translations are below.

From the west end fireplace: *"Freedom, honor, loyalty and farther."*

"Those are my principles when I look back at my life," says Duffeler, recalling a college English assignment when he had to make a personal shield and created the German motto for it.

From the east end fireplace: *"Do things right and let people talk."*

Wessex Hall, South view.

This one stems from Duffeler's father, a publisher, who shared those 13th century words with his son. The idea is to do things the right way all the time and let the chips fall where they will.

"That's a wonderful concept," Duffeler says. "Let people talk. They'll say whatever they like."

Hush, Listen and Discover the Magic Alongside the Williamsburg Winery Duck Pond

The Williamsburg Winery founder Patrick Duffeler makes no secret of how frequently nature inspires him. He favors the tranquility and restorative qualities even a simple walk outside can provide. No wonder he recollects with vigor his endeavor to clear the overgrowth surrounding an underused pond.

Today the Williamsburg Winery Duck Pond is another spot on the 300-acre Wessex Hundred farm to casually enjoy wine.

Just a few paces away from the raised lawn behind the winery, the Duck Pond is something of a hidden gem, a place to "relax or propose!" Patrick's wife, Françoise, remarks with a glimmer in her eyes.

Both have been done alongside the elongated pond that includes its own small island.

The Duck Pond dates to the effort to modernize the roadways for easier access to the winery in the 1990s. Back then, the pines that now stand 45 feet tall were only seedlings.

At one point, Duffeler surrounded the water with a split-rail oak fence that later eroded and was torn down.

"The ducks loved it more than the geese," he says. "It wasn't large enough for the geese."

For years, the pond was ignored, "even by myself," Duffeler admits.

That changed last winter after a conversation to bring in heavy equipment to remove the thicket. That idea didn't sit well with the elder Duffeler, particular about every aspect of

A new Muscat vineyard planted just south of the Duck Pond.

the Williamsburg Winery.

"I'll do it," he announced. "It was a jungle. There were wild grapevines. I'm not fond of wild grapevines."

Duffeler swapped his business suit for fatigues every Sunday and joined four from the winery's viticultural crew to clear the space.

To reiterate, his role wasn't a supervisory one.

"We were working together as five equals," he says.

As taxing as taming the neglected vines proved, the results rewarded the labor.

Now complete, the Duck Pond offers another place to pause, whether you're walking with a wine glass in hand or are on bended knee for a significant request.

Visitors are encouraged to spread out a blanket or enjoy one of the recently added white picnic tables.

Expect daffodils to color the banks again this spring. Trees and plants, selected by Duffeler, accentuate this peaceful space. Excess algae in the water has been removed along with any remnants of those dastardly wild grapevines and other parasites such as poison ivy, poison oak, and others.

As marvelous of a retreat as it is for visitors, the pond that is 6 to 8 feet deep in spots is home to flocks of ducks and other species. They live carelessly here.

A duck in descent produces another of nature's most exquisite sounds. Listen closely to the chatter of waterfowl that is a harmonious conversation all by itself, and all of life's other noises fade into the background.

Revel in Wonderful Westbury Hall

Intimate. Charming. Picturesque.

Westbury Hall at the Williamsburg Winery shares those qualities with its namesake, the village of Westbury in southwest England.

The three-level converted warehouse opens into a multipurpose space on the main floor perfect for hosting a wedding. Upon entry, the eye easily finds the sweeping oak staircase, designed with a bride in mind. The landing with the shield of Westbury as a backdrop makes for a marvelous moment to pause and snap a keepsake photo.

"It allows for a dramatic walking down the stairs," says Patrick Duffeler, founder of the Williamsburg Winery

An upstairs bridal suite painted a warm coral color welcomes the bride and her party to tend to the final details. Patrick's wife, Françoise, chose the inviting palette.

But Westbury Hall is suitable for more than weddings.

Businessmen and -women will feel at home here, too. The White Horse Meeting Room offers space beyond the typical corporate board room starting with the atypical conference table. Six separate tables made from exotic Indonesian wood form one large rectangular table; a projection screen can be raised or lowered depending on needs. Engravings that date to the 18th century, each hand selected by the Duffelers, are framed on the walls.

Who would not be stimulated sitting inside this space brightened by natural light?

An aside on the choosing of White Horse to name the meeting room: if you know Patrick Duffeler, you know it wasn't an arbitrary decision. What's known as the Westbury White Horse, carved into chalk grassland in the late 1600s in Wiltshire, by some accounts symbolizes a victorious King Alfred the Great in battle. White horses are scattered throughout English hillsides. The white horse is also tied to a favorite book of Duffeler's, "Far from the Madding Crowd," written by Thomas Hardy in 1874.

"It actually takes place in Wessex," says Duffeler, whose extensive personal library includes a book on the significance of the white horse in British history.

Notice the intentional alliteration of all the W's on the the 300-acre farm Duffeler called Wessex Hundred. The hotel on the grounds is Wedmore Place; the largest venue is Wessex Hall, which spills into Westbury Hall. White Horse Meeting Room. The Williamsburg Winery.

"Consistency matters," Duffeler says.

The hallways that connect the upstairs rooms display more collectibles from Europe, including a French grape harvest basket from the late 18th century given to us by our friend Jim Raper.

Downstairs, a 40-seat private tasting area with a view of the wine cellar allows enthusiasts to sample new and familiar offerings.

A walk into the actual cellar, chilly at 62 degrees, is a treat heightened by the classical music at a pleasant volume on a continuous loop. It's dim yet brightened with just enough glow by petite globes, helpful for meandering past the stacked barrels of wine without hesitation.

"We're looking to expand this area," Duffeler says. Currently, the cellar holds well over 600 barrels of wine; he'd prefer it be 1,000.

Most of the cellar looks exactly as you'd imagine, with barrels upon barrels of reserve wine. The occasional moisture on the floor stems from excessive humidity in the walls. Filtration and fermentation equipment serve as reminders of how complex winemaking is. Minus the tasting room, some areas of the cellar is not open for guests.

A trek back up the stairs returns you to the open space where many brides and grooms have pledged their "I do's." Tapestries and other relics enhance Westbury Hall. Among the more striking pieces: a china cabinet standing 7 feet tall from The Périgord, an enchanting region in southwest France that sweeps visitors up with its lore. An armoire adorned with diamond shape geometric designs reminiscent of Louis XIII features marvelous craftwork.

The idyllic village of Westbury is a treasure in the United Kingdom. So, too, is Westbury Hall at the Williamsburg Winery.

The great stairway from the bride's room to Westbury Hall.

Sip the Wine, Savor the View, Stick Around for a While at the 1619 Pavilion

Fresh air, a vineyard view, relaxed seating. The 1619 Pavilion at the Williamsburg Winery offers another setting for what founder Patrick Duffeler calls "the casual enjoyment of wine."

The two-level, 2,600 square-foot deck that opened in spring 2019 overlooks a pair of vineyards. The upstairs and downstairs offer ample seating, and if it's chilly, request your own personal heater for a little extra toastiness.

A dog- and kid-friendly terrace and a fire pit are more amenities. That leaves plenty of options to enjoy a flight or a glass of wine and nibble on the bites from the Gabriel Archer Tavern. The bar is staffed on the lower level. The upper deck is reserved for guests 21 and older.

Like everything at the Williamsburg Winery, the 1619 Pavilion has a story behind its name. The House of Burgesses at their first gathering and expression of democratic assembly in the English world required colonists to grow grapes and make wine under The Acte 12 of 1619.

"The House of Burgesses said everybody should have a vineyard, and I'm one of the ones still following the rules of 1619!" Duffeler quipped.

When the Pavilion opened in spring 2019, it marked the 400th anniversary of the Acte. It also represents another evolution of the winery, which opened in 1985 and later added Wedmore Place, Wessex Hall and Westbury Hall.

Duffeler observed over the years that some visitors wanted to experiencie the Williamsburg Winery while remaining on the grounds of the Wessex Hundred farm. The 1619 Pavilion is an extension of that idea.

The comfy cushioned chairs and rockers invite visitors to stay as long as they would like and savor the nearby Albariño and Petit vineyards.

Live music and wine-by-the-glass specials were part of the Pavilion's inaugural summer and will continue once COVID-19 restrictions lift.

History buffs might consider this for a special toast —uncork a bottle of the 2019 Acte 12 of 1619 Chardonnay that features flavors of golden apple, toasted marshmallow and cinnamon-dusted puff pastry among others. Enjoy the dry yet fruity sweetness relaxing at the 1619 Pavilion.

The 1619 Pavilion reminding visitors of the Acte 12 of 1619 of the Burgesses in Jamestown that was the first assembly in English America.

Wedmore Place Brings Europe to Williamsburg

Traveling unlocks the adventurer in us and stimulates our natural curiosity to learn about the customs and cultures of somewhere new.

Wedmore Place, the hotel at the Williamsburg Winery, invites guests to discover a different part of Europe with every new stay.

Each of the 28 rooms reflects a theme reinforced with appropriate antiques and works of art. All come with wood-burning fireplaces. The comfortable robes in each room are enticing to cozy up to the warmth with a glass of wine before enjoying a restful night's sleep in a king-sized bed. The names of the rooms correspond to the regions they represent — Scandinavia, Brandenburg, and Tuscany, to list a few.

Like everything on Wessex Hundred, Wedmore Place is rooted in history. Patrick Duffeler, founder of the Williamsburg Winery, wanted to create a European style hotel, similar to one in Nuits-Saint-Georges in northern Burgundy, where he overnighted multiple times while working for a Geneva-based investment group decades ago.

"It was a wonderful place. It exuded warmth. It exuded history," he says. "It was comfortable. It was traditional and it was unique. These are all the things I like in a hotel."

And here's what he doesn't like. Back in the early '70s, he logged more than 200 flights per year as the developer of the Formula 1 motor racing team. Waking up in a standardized room devoid of character, he'd initially wonder, "Am I in Cincinnati or Singapore?"

"These hotels, they are all the same. They had no soul, no history," he says.

During Duffeler's early visits to Williamsburg — starting with his first in 1961 as a recent high school graduate and including several with his parents — he felt the historic district and surrounding area needed a better hotel.

The initial design for Wedmore Place was made in 1989. Two years later, Duffeler brought aboard John Hopke, the Williamsburg architect behind all of the Williamsburg Winery's major construction projects.

The entrance to the lobby in Wedmore Place.

149

Duffeler hit the pause button due to the savings and loan crisis and recession in real estate that consumed much of the 1990s. The ground for Wedmore Place was broken in 2005.

As suggested by Patrick II, the founder's son, the hotel derives its name from a nineth-century agreement between King Alfred of Wessex and the Danish leader Guthrum to prevent future military conflict. The Treaty of Wedmore set up geographical boundaries that led to peace in the area.

"We adopted the name Wedmore because I wanted Wedmore Place to be a peaceful place," Duffeler says.

The sounds from Wedmore Place relate to its natural wooded surroundings far from the rumble of the interstate.

The hotel opened in 2007 with Gerald Baliles in attendance. The former Virginia Governor was also on hand for the launch of the Williamsburg Winery 22 years earlier.

"When we opened on October 7, Jerry and his wife, Robin, stayed overnight in the Venetian Suite," says Duffeler, referring to the largest of the hotel's rooms, with more than 1,100 square feet.

Duffeler and his wife, Françoise, handpicked the tapestries, antiques and furnishings that make each room inside Wedmore Place distinct. The pillars at the entrance to the lobby came from France as did the frame to the front door and each of the outdoor fountains.

"We bought antiques from Scandinavia, antiques from Holland, Germany, Belgium, Italy, Spain and France," Duffeler said. "We gathered them all in the warehouse of an Alsatian antique dealer in Provence. He was a charming man who stored them for us."

They were shipped in a large container to Newport News, and the Duffelers decided what would go where.

All of the rooms "are my favorites," Duffeler said.

Even the hallways are special, reminiscent of a walk through the Louvre. Shields from each of the 28 regions are on display in the lobby. Tapestries and period paintings decorate the hallways.

The staff takes pride in its hospitality that centers on pampering. With 31 open hearth fireplaces through Wedmore Place's rooms and shared spaces, guests will experience warm during their respite there.

The true adventurer will take advantage of the Wedmore Place passport. If a guest visits 27 times and chooses a different room for every stay, the 28th time is free.

"We give them a complete passport — hand stamped on every page," Duffeler says.

The Williamsburg Winery owner is regularly asked how old the building is. When he replies that it was built in 2007, guests appear stunned.

"They think of it as being an old building," he says. "That's a compliment for me. We wanted to give it a unique feel. The wonderful thing is people come over to celebrate an event and then they come back to celebrate it again. They say, 'I just love this place.' And I love that."

Revel in the Gabriel Archer Tavern, a Welcome Respite with a Storied History

"Hello! Welcome!"

The frequent greetings from Patrick Duffeler turns some heads as he walks through the Gabriel Archer Tavern on the grounds of the winery and farm he founded decades ago.

The founder of the Williamsburg Winery makes a point to make an appearance to welcome guests, not to disturb them.

Because welcome is how he wants them all to feel. It's how he's always wanted the community to feel.

And relaxed.

Whether sitting inside the Gabriel Archer Tavern, the winery's French-inspired full-service eatery, or outside on the red brick underneath a splendid wisteria canopy, know this: While savoring a bottle of wine — paired with homemade pimento cheese, Prince Edward Island steamed mussels or any of the other delights on the menu — the sounds you hear will stem from your own conversation.

The view from your window seat or patio chair will be of vineyards in varying stages of growth depending on the time of year.

The noise and the exhaust of tractor-trailers and other engines rumbling through Williamsburg on Interstate 64 is nine miles away, but it might as well be 100.

Gabriel Archer Tavern is a restorative sanctuary, ideal for reflection or catching up with friends. No one is in a rush leave because it is so pleasant to stay.

"The Tavern has been very popular from day one," says Belgium-born Duffeler, whose vision for a winery in Colonial Williamsburg wasn't shared by many back in the early '80s. "It's contributed to the businesses and revenues of the company and it's created a concept. You can sit outdoors. You turn all around, and you just see green space."

It was Duffeler's business acumen and much of his own physical labor that transformed

The main room at the Gabriel Archer Tavern featuring the old cypress planks, compliments of our friend Rob Bickford.

what he describes as "a mess" into the state's largest winery. Credit the lush backdrop to Duffeler, too. He's planted 62,000 trees in 300-acre Wessex Hundred Farm. A good day for Duffeler combines green space and fresh air — slowing down to tune in the sounds of nature as one of his favorite books, "The Secret Life of Trees," recommends.

History is important to him, too, and you'll find it everywhere at Gabriel Archer Tavern, a former tractor shed that he had a hand in constructing.

The 60x24-foot shed was built in September 1987, replacing a dilapidated barn, and was actually a multipurpose facility of sorts. In addition to housing tractors and equipment, it provided a comfortable upstairs apartment for Jeanette Smith, the winery's first viticultural manager.

But when winery construction was in its infancy, Duffeler learned that in order to meet federal requirements for licensing, he needed a designated bonding area. The shed met those expectations and the Williamsburg Winery became officially licensed on Nov. 24, 1987.

As plans moved forward, the license was formally transferred from the shed to the winery. When Smith moved on, the shed was no longer needed, but Duffeler decided not to tear it down.

Duffeler didn't immediately warm up to the idea of serving food on the grounds; his director of consumer activities, Drew Haynie, proposed the idea in the early '90s.

"We should do something to elevate the enjoyment of people," Haynie suggested. "How about doing a restaurant?"

"I don't want to do a restaurant," Duffeler responded.

"How about a place for small food and the opportunity for people to sit down and get a glass of wine?" Haynie asked.

"Drew, you're on!" Duffeler said.

The tractor shed needed modification, starting with replacing the concrete floor with a wooden one made from the richest of cedar planks. Initially, Duffeler used the space to welcome close friends and serve them fresh food from the commercial kitchen. When the Gabriel Archer Tavern opened to the public in 1996, the menu featured largely tapas along with multiple wine selections.

Today its lunch and dinner menus are eclectic, though nothing outsells the turkey and brie sandwich, distinct thanks to the Lingonberry preserves and roasted garlic mayo that complement house-roasted turkey brined for a week. The savory and salty mix atop the crusty French bread pairs well with a Chardonnay from the winery.

From the crepe myrtles that line the winery entrance to the inaugural label, Governor's White, every facet of the winery is purposeful, including the choice to name the tavern in honor of Gabriel Archer.

"The Williamsburg Winery, in every dimension, has to reflect the history of Virginia," said Duffeler, who refers to Williamsburg as "the soul of America."

Cambridge-educated Archer, one of Jamestown's most significant early leaders, co-captained the Godspeed, the lead ship among three vessels that brought the men who founded the first permanent settlement in the English New World. The explorers considered multiple sites near the Chesapeake Bay, but fearful of pirates, looked inland to establish a colony for The Virginia Company, a private venture under a Royal Charter.

Archer envisioned locating the settlement at the mouth of a creek that was to be named Archer's Hope — hope referred to an "opening or hollow amongst hills." Capt. John Smith overruled the idea and placed the settlement on Jamestown Island.

But Duffeler was inspired by Archer's preference to place the first settlement on what today is part of the farm; he named his first "reserve" wine the Gabriel Archer Reserve.

A rustic signpost that greets Tavern visitors features the Godspeed.

In 2004, the tavern expanded the kitchen, added a vineyard room that brings the outdoors in and added capacity for private dining.

"The Tavern became a popular place," said Duffeler, who enjoys lunch there frequently with his wife, Françoise. She enjoys the soups and salads most while he goes for a charcuterie board.

Duffeler also added a tiled counter with tall seats, similar to an upscale bar.

Tavern décor once included a replica of Colonial ships courtesy of The Mariners Museum. It's a whimsical mix inside now, including pottery that features Duffeler's designs, wooden tables and chairs and overhead lighting fixtures featuring modified wine bottles as shades. Colonial agricultural tools are on display, including an old press from an auction.

Outdoors, wind chimes respond to the gentle breeze. Flowerpots grow marigolds and the herbs incorporated into many of the dishes. Every dish features at least one local component.

Duffeler considers the tavern a world onto itself. It's a place to focus on relationships rather than the screen of a cell phone. He invites you to sip, savor and soak in the inviting respite, an elegant but understated retreat that enchants longtime locals and first-time visitors alike.

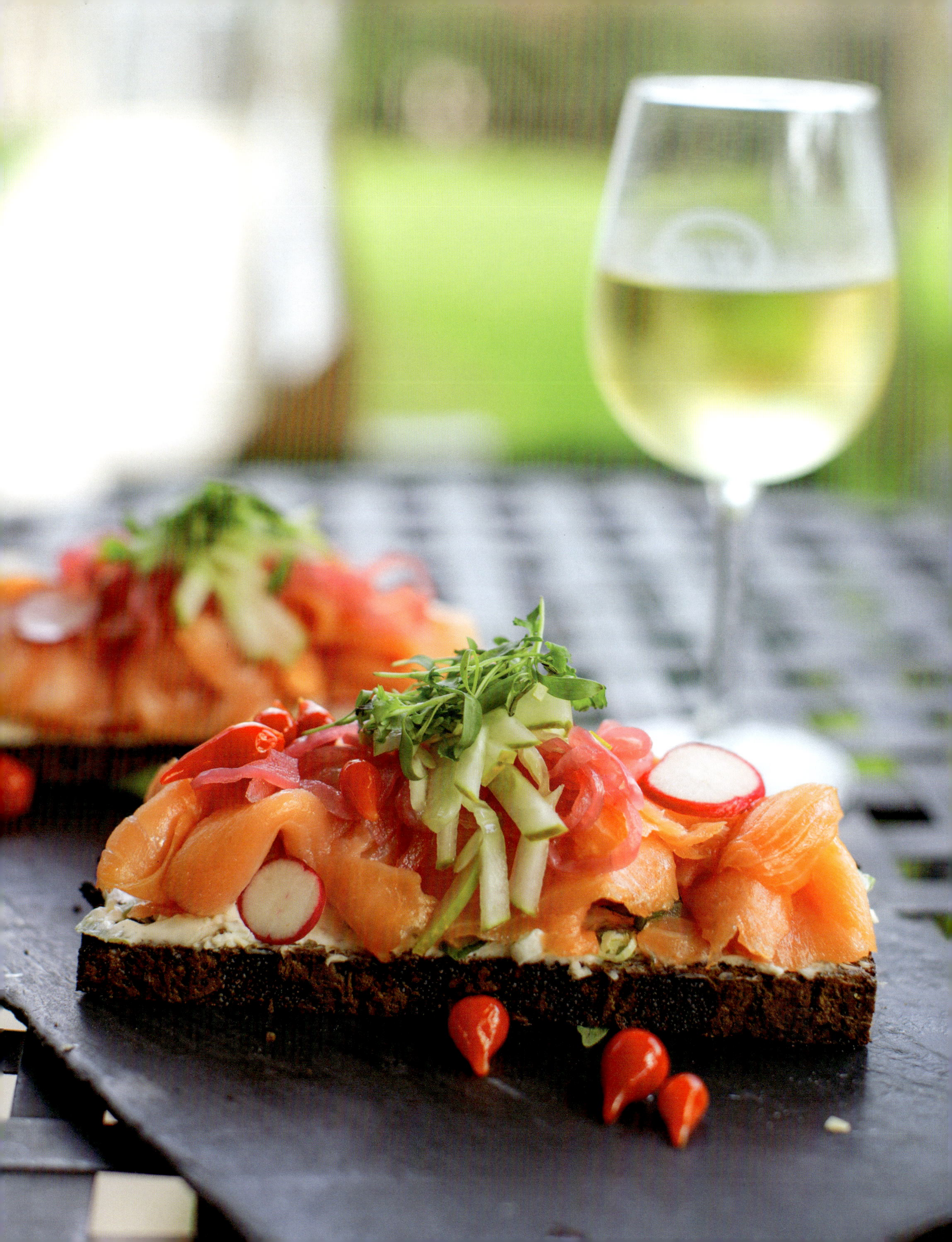

Merchants Square Wine Bar and Tasting Room an Extension of the Warmth Found at Wessex Hundred

Visitors to Wessex Hundred can savor their Williamsburg Winery flight at multiple spots on the farm — the Gabriel Archer Tavern, the 1619 Pavilion and the Duck Pond to name a few.

They are far removed from the daily buzz found at a commercial area.

Counter that with a stop at the Williamsburg Winery Tasting Room and Wine Bar at Merchants Square – which is equally as pleasant in its own way.

The 18th-century style retail village located adjacent to Colonial Williamsburg, features more than 40 shops, and it bustles. Specialty stores invite browsing, and on a seasonal day, the brick-lined widened walkway swells with people of all ages enjoying the historic district.

You'll find the Williamsburg Winery's bar and tasting room at 427 Duke of Gloucester St., tucked between The Precious Gem and R. Bryant, Ltd menswear shop. The satellite location opened in 2017.

"There are easily a million people a year walking down Duke of Gloucester Street," said Patrick Duffeler, founder of the Williamsburg Winery.

That's a captive audience, many of whom haven't discovered the charms of Wessex Hundred. A visit to the wine bar ideally encourages them to check it out firsthand. But for those who have eaten at Gabriel Archer Tavern or stayed at Wedmore Place, the hotel on the grounds of the farm, the wine bar is a pleasing reminder of the larger operation.

Wine Club members receive 20% off of every flight.

"I want to be cordial. I want to be hospitable," Duffeler said. "I want to extend those relationships we've already made."

Sharing conversation over wine connects people and nurtures friendships; the Merchants Square location offers opportunity for both.

Albeit a mere 1,300 square feet, the wine bar offers a deceiving amount of spots for the casual enjoyment of a glass or flight of wine. A small plates menu of local cheese and charcuterie refreshes any weary visitor.

Step through the brick-lined archway, climb the winding sets of stairs, and immediately, you're whisked into a quaint setting with ample options for sitting or standing, as many prefer. Comfy spaces with pillows beckon as do the various types of tables. Longer rectangular ones can accommodate a group. Smaller circular tables lend themselves to more intimate chatter. Additional crevices with window views relax the solo wine drinker.

Outdoor seating is hard to resist when the weather is right.

The hard part is selecting a flight. The options are a Wessex Hundred Flight, a Virginia Sweets Flight and a Sparking Flight along with flights of all reds or whites and even a Cider Flight. Of course, bottles are available to share on the premises or to take home for another occasion.

Wine-inspired décor and fixtures add to the ambiance as does background classical music. A chalkboard featuring simplistic but precise drawings of vines adds a touch of whimsy to the space.

Duffeler repeats one of his favorite mottos etched on the east end wall of Wessex Hall when asked about the success of the tasting room and wine bar.

Do things right and let people talk.

No doubt, they'll have plenty of good things to say.

The outlet in an attractive retail center in Virginia Beach. It was opened in late 2019.

Some of the many associates who get the job done at the Winery or at the hotel. From left to right – Row 1: Kelly Mierle- Functions and Debra Kidney- Retail Shops Manager. Row 2: Bob Davis- Winemaking and Maintenance, Leah Robertson- Functions, Sonny Pickens- Bottling Supervisor, and Wes Mazah- Sous Chef. Row 3: Karen Hobler- Wedmore Place Manager, John Goff- Wedmore Place Maintenance, Josh Hutter- Chef de Cuisine. Row 4: Randy Campbell- Warehouse and Distribution Manager, Steve Stalnaker- Assistant Manager Retail Shop, and Stacey Lightfoot Winelab and Assistant Winemaker.

To explore the Williamsburg Winery through stories
and photos further, visit williamsburgwinery.com.

There, you'll find even more details about the wines from Wessex Hundred, year-by-year history of the farm from the words of Founder Patrick Duffeler, visual tours through the rooms of Wedmore Place, details about how to join the wine club, information about upcoming events, and more.

EPILOGUE

There are seemingly countless variables affecting every step associated with the growing and making of wine. They have been presented in this document in the hopes that they will open the door to a better understanding of the vast range of aromas and flavors that are released during the winemaking process and continue to evolve in the barrel and in the bottle. This delivery in itself is what confuses some, impresses others, and fascinates many.

All those who enjoy drinking wine have read the opinions expressed by the experts. A high profile retailer or famous restauranteur who goes to France may be extraordinarily well received by several of the thousands of wine producers in that country. This traveler may come back with impressions that were impacted as much by the charm of his hosts or the beauty of the scenery as by the wines themselves. Do these wines all travel well? Usually, but not always.

Some producers in Europe go so far as to prepare special "cuvées," or blends, for the American market, in hopes of winning the favor of someone like Robert Parker, probably our best-known wine expert. The fact is, not all experts have the same palate or the same opinions. I have seen widely varying verdicts on the same wine handed down by equally qualified professionals.

Masters of Wine and Master Sommeliers are the PhDs of the wine world. They are people who have dedicated their lives to the study, appreciation, and tasting of an enormous array of wines, and they sit on the panels at many wine competitions. At some events, I have seen these judges exposed to as many as a hundred wines, which had to be tasted in a single morning. That is unfortunate, simply because palate fatigue does occur, and the ability to truly appreciate the flavor and aroma components of a wine declines after a person has tasted twenty-five to thirty entries. More importantly, these wines are judged without food, the boon companion for which wine was intended in the first place.

While I recognize the significant contribution to the wine industry of many of the experts, a lot of what is written needs to be taken with a measure of good humor and with the same caution that should accompany any opinion—on food in a restaurant, for example—that is based on individual taste.

While it can certainly be enjoyed by itself, without question, wine was meant as an accompaniment to food and serves us best when taken with a meal. Almost as much as the wine itself, I personally value the table settings, the presentation of dishes, the quality and style of the glass into which the wine is poured, and that the glass is filled to the correct level to permit one to gently swirl the wine in order to release and savor its bouquet before tasting. Most of all, I value the ambiance and the company and the occasions which allow us to celebrate that beverage, which for thousands of years, has contributed so much to the enjoyment of a full and happy life.

As I see it, a good wine is purely an expression of what Nature offers us.

Enjoy Life,

Patrick and Françoise Duffeler